THE DANIEL PARALLEL
A CLEAR AND PRESENT TRUTH REFERENCE GUIDE

■ *Bible (KJV)*   ■ *Daniel Commentary*   ■ *E.G. White Notes*   ■ *Paraphrase*

Rapid Movements Publishing
Hampton, GA 30228

Copyright © 2021 by Tory St.Cyr

Printed in the United States of America

All Rights Reserved

Published by Rapid Movements Publishing
Hampton, GA 30228

Other books by Tory St.Cyr may be purchased at www.clearandpresenttruth.com

The author assumes full responsibility for the accuracy of all facts and quotations, as cited in this book.

ISBN: 978-1-7366073-5-0

Pictures and Illustrations

Babylonian Captivity By derivative work: Steerpike (talk)Arc_de_Triumph_copy.jpg: user: בית השלום - Arc_de_Triumph_copy.jpg, CC BY 3.0, https://commons.wikimedia.org/w/index.php?curid=4303855

By After Briton Rivière - Manchester City Art Gallery [sic!], Public Domain, https://commons.wikimedia.org/w/index.php?curid=50214

These digitally adjusted compilations of them the copyright of FreeBibleimages. Artist Jim Padgett. They are made available for free download under a Creative Commons Attribution-ShareAlike 3.0 Unported license.

https://www.cgtrader.com/

Freepik.com

Fiverr.com (pro_design_up)

Goodsalt.com

This book is dedicated to my Father Davy St.Cyr. You are the one who taught me everything I know about the Bible and whose footsteps I have followed in studying, teaching, and writing books on Bible prophecy. Thank you for being a teacher, a mentor, and a friend. I love you.

TABLE OF CONTENTS

Acknowledgments	9
Preface	11
The Babylonian Captivity	15
The Image of the Past, Present, and Future	27
The Fiery Trial of the Three Hebrews	53
The Humbling of King Nebuchadnezzar	73
The Handwriting on the Wall	95
Daniel in the Lion's Den	117
The Animalistic Attributes of the Four Kingdoms	139
The Cleansing of the Sanctuary	169
The Seventy-Weeks Prophecy	195
Daniel's Final Vision	219
The Final War	235
Three Prophetic Periods	283
Test Your Knowledge Questions and Answers	301
Topical Index	307

ACKNOWLEDGMENTS

I would like to acknowledge my debt of gratitude to everyone who contributed to the success of this book.

My lovely wife, Gina essentially became a single parent while I spent many days and nights cooped up in my office researching, typing, and praying. She not only kept the house going, but also pushed me to continue writing when I wanted to give up. I love you, Babe.

I also wish to express thanks to my two incredible sons, Joshua and Jonathan, who would sometimes pray for me during worship when I remarked that I was stuck on a particular verse in this book. I love you both.

I would be remiss if I were to skip over my loving mom, Retha. She always sounded so enthusiastic whenever I gave her an update on where I was in my process of writing this book. I love you, Mom.

I would also like to thank all my closest friends (you know who you are) who helped me in a myriad of ways—from making suggestions to this book, to helping me decide on a name for it; I want to express my gratitude for all the ways you showed me your support. I love you all.

Lastly, the greatest acknowledgment goes to my Lord and Savior Jesus Christ, Who is the inspiration behind this book. Thank you, Lord, for being patient with me and encouraging me, even though I didn't deserve it. I love You.

PREFACE

The Book of Daniel has been one of my favorite books from the time I was a child. I can still remember going up to the front of the church for children's story, and no matter how many times the storyteller used Daniel as the lesson, I always enjoyed it. I mean, who didn't love to hear Daniel lasting a whole night in that lion's den? I would sit there and imagine the look on the faces of Daniel's accusers when they found out Daniel was still alive. And what about the three Hebrew boys? They stood in the face of death and didn't even break a sweat! (Yes, there was a little pun intended). The point is, I stayed in the safe story zones of Daniel and never ventured into the difficult prophecy zones, with the beasts and the horns—simply because I felt that it was just too hard to understand.

My dad, who was an elder, studied prophecy in great depth and with great passion and would often speak on the book of Revelation when he had the opportunity to preach in church. In fact, this happened so often that he became known as the "Prophecy Elder." And since I was his son, many assumed that if the father understood prophecy—well, his son must understand it too. And so, my journey to understanding prophecy began.

This journey started with me asking my dad questions about prophecy. Then I read Ellen White's *The Great Controversy* and Uriah Smith's *Daniel and the Revelation.* As it turned out, the more I read, the more God would allow me to comprehend. And the more I comprehended, the more I began to appreciate those beasts, horns, and time prophecies. As a matter of fact, I started enjoying it so much that I forgot about the Daniel of the lion's den and primarily focused on Daniel the prophet!

However, when discussing these prophecies with my fellow church members, I discovered that most people had the same hang-ups that I'd previously had with Daniel. They didn't want to venture out of the safe story zones. As a result, I suggested to some that they should look for a plain English Bible translation. To others, I suggested consulting a commentary to help break down the interpretation of specific verses. And to a few, I recommended Ellen White's commentary on Daniel, as she provides insight that's often overlooked. Essentially, I suggested three different resources to help them better understand Daniel.

Then it occurred to me— What if I combined those three resources into *one* resource? What if I could create a one-stop-shop parallel on the Book of Daniel? This is where *The Daniel Parallel* comes in.

If you allow it, I believe this book will not only bless you in understanding the prophecies of Daniel, but it will also give you the tools to teach prophecy to others. You may not agree with everything I've written, but by the grace of God, you'll be able to understand it. God bless you.

Bible (King James Version)

This first column of this book will contain Scriptures from Daniel taken directly from the Authorized King James Version (KJV) translation. While there are other quality translations of God's Word, I chose the KJV because it's still one of the most commonly used versions of the Bible and is typically accepted by most Christians even if they prefer another version.

The Bible is our standard. Everything written in this parallel study book must be examined against the Word of God to ensure it agrees. If there is anything written in this book that is contrary to Scripture, you must reject it.

There are two main reasons that we look to the prophecies in Scripture:

(1) To remind us that Jesus is soon to return
(2) To allow us to see the validity of the Bible and believe

This is why prophecy is so powerful!

As we strive to understand the prophecies in the Book of Daniel, we will see that God has revealed to us the events that precede the end of the world.

However, we must always be mindful that simply knowing how the world ends *without* knowing Jesus will not save us.

My prayer is that, as you read this book, you will see Jesus in these pages and know He truly loves you.

Daniel Commentary

In this second column, you will find Bible commentary that corresponds with the verses found in the first column.

What is a Bible commentary?
A Bible commentary is a sentence, a paragraph, or an entire book that explains the meaning of Scripture passages. Bible commentaries typically provide the reader with a little more context to help the reader understand the meaning of the text(s) in question. Commentaries are often based on the author's perspective; however, the author is also expected to provide support for that perspective.

With that being said, the majority of the commentary in this column is influenced by the ideas expressed in the *Seventh-day Adventist Bible Commentary*. However, certain portions of the commentary provided in this column will differ from the views expressed in the Seventh-day Adventist Bible Commentary. In these situations, please keep in mind that whenever I take a position that might be considered atypical to Seventh-day Adventists, both of the following will be true:

(1) I don't entirely agree with the explanation expressed in the Seventh-day Adventist Commentary.
(2) The Spirit of Prophecy (i.e., the writings of E. G. White) is either vague or altogether silent on the subject.

When these two situations occur, I will provide an alternative view along with the reason why that view was preferred.

Therefore, commentary in this column should not be considered as a substitute for the official Seventh-day Adventist Bible commentary on Daniel.

Please note: At times, the commentary in this column will skip a verse. This omission is by design and will only occur if I believe the verse is self-explanatory.

E.G. White Notes

Ellen G. White (EGW) was an individual who lived most of her life during the 1800s. From the time she was 17, the Lord began giving her visions and dreams. These visions and dreams, covering a wide range of topics, became the basis for much of her writings. Seventh-day Adventists believe Ellen White had the gift of prophecy and view her writings as inspired.

EGW's writings provide further information and commentary on what has already been revealed in Scripture. However, EGW's writings are not on par with the Bible and should never be used in that fashion. She said it best herself when she said, "Scripture is God's Revelation, I recommend to you, dear reader, the Word of God as the rule of your faith and practice. By that Word we are to be judged." *Early Writings p. 78.*

I have provided quotations from some of her books and articles in this third column that correlates with the Scripture and commentary in the first two columns.

Below is a list of the abbreviated EGW sources and the full book names that correlate to them:

1BC	Bible Commentary, The SDA , Vol. #
1888 GC	Great Controversy, The (1888 Edition)
1MR	Manuscript Releases, Vol. #
1SM	Selected Messages, Book #
1SP	Spirit of Prophecy, The, Vol. #
1T	Testimonies for the Church Vol. #
CCh	Counsels for the Church
CM	Colporteur Ministry
DA	Desire of Ages, The
EW	Early Writings
FCE	Fundamentals of Christian Education
FSTS	From Splendor to Shadow
GC	Great Controversy, The
LDE	Last Day Events
Lt	Letter, E. G. White
ML	My Life Today
Ms	Manuscript, E. G. White
PaM	Pastoral Ministry
PK	Prophets and Kings
PP	Patriarchs and Prophets
RH	Review and Herald
SL	Sanctified Life
SR	Story of Redemption, The
ST	Signs of the Times
TM	Testimonies to Ministers and Gospel Workers
YI	Youth's Instructor

The Clear and Present Paraphrase

What is a paraphrase?

In the purest sense of the word, paraphrasing is to express the meaning of something written or spoken using different words to achieve greater clarity.

That being said, I have created my own Daniel paraphrase for the sole purpose of expressing what I believe the book of Daniel is telling us. In this, I hope that you will gain further clarity for yourself.

As with any paraphrase, the information in this column is not a translation of the Bible like the KJV or NIV. Nevertheless, this paraphrase intends to provide you, the reader, a verse-by-verse easy reader that makes the Scriptures as plain as possible.

This column essentially is a culmination of:

1. The format and foundation of the Scriptures found in the first column.
2. The additional context provided by the commentary found in the second column.
3. And the added insight provided by Ellen White found in the third column.

All of this is neatly packaged for you in a clear and concise manner so you can see how each verse of this paraphrase is derived.

The inspiration for this paraphrase comes from a complete Bible paraphrase called *The Clear Word* by Jack Blanco.

While our writing styles differ in regard to the level of detail provided, *The Clear Word* was one of the reasons I decided to write this book, and it was always at arm's length of me during the writing process.

And one day, I hope someone like you will decide to write a book on Daniel...and I can only hope that *The Daniel Parallel* will be at your arm's length.

Daniel, Shadrach, Meshach, and Abednego are faced with the tough decision to either eat the King's meat or follow God's plan.

Daniel 1

The Babylonian Captivity

KJV Bible

CHAPTER 1

1. In the third year of the reign of Jehoiakim king of Judah came Nebuchadnezzar king of Babylon unto Jerusalem, and besieged it.
2. And the Lord gave Jehoiakim king of Judah into his hand, with part of the vessels of the house of God: which he carried into the land of Shinar to the house of his god; and he brought the vessels into the treasure house of his god.
3. And the king spake unto Ashpenaz the master of his eunuchs, that he should bring *certain* of the children of Israel, and of the king's seed, and of the princes;
4. Children in whom *was* no blemish, but well favoured, and skilful in all wisdom, and cunning in knowledge, and understanding science, and such as *had* ability in them to stand in the king's palace, and whom they might teach the learning and the tongue of the Chaldeans.
5. And the king appointed them a daily provision of the king's meat, and of the wine which he drank: so nourishing them three years, that at the end thereof they might stand before the king.

Daniel Commentary

CHAPTER 1

1. **The third Year** - Jehoiakim's 3rd year as ruler lasted, by the Jewish calendar, from 606 BC to the autumn of 605 BC. It appears that the events recorded must have taken place sometime during the Jewish civil year that began in the fall of 606 BC. **King of Babylon** - When Nebuchadnezzar came against Jerusalem in Jehoiakim's 3rd year, he was not yet the king; however, Daniel most likely recorded these events after Nebuchadnezzar became king, hence the name "king of Babylon."
2. **Land of Shinar** - In many of the OT references, Shinar is a term for Babylonia. **His god** - The chief god of the Babylonians was Marduk, who was also known as *Bêl*.
3. **King's seed** - It was customary for conquerors to carry away royal hostages to guarantee the loyalty of those who were conquered.
4. **No Blemish** - Physically sound with a handsome form were considered essential qualities to high-rank officers. **Chaldeans** - A class of scholars at the Babylonian court
5. **Provision of the king's meat** - "portion" or "delicacies."

EG White Notes

CHAPTER 1

In the land of their captivity these men were to carry out God's purpose by giving to heathen nations the blessings that come through a knowledge of Jehovah. *PK 479*

The king did not compel the Hebrew youth to renounce their faith in favor of idolatry, but he hoped to bring this about gradually. By giving them names significant of idolatry, by bringing them daily into close association with idolatrous customs, and under the influence of the seductive rites of heathen worship, he hoped to induce them to renounce the religion of their nation and to unite with the worship of the Babylonians. *PK 481*

The fact that these men, worshipers of Jehovah, were captives in Babylon, and that the vessels of God's house had been placed in the Temple of the Babylonish gods, was boastfully cited by the victors as evidence that their religion and customs were superior to the religion and customs of the Hebrews.

God gave Babylon evidence of His supremacy, of the holiness of His requirements, and of the sure results of obedience. *PK 480-481*

The Clear and Present Paraphrase

CHAPTER 1

1. In Jehoiakim's third year as ruler of Judah, King Nebuchadnezzar, who, at that time was the Prince of Babylon, comes to Jerusalem with an army and surrounds the city.

2. Unfortunately for Jehoiakim, the Lord chooses not to intervene on his behalf, and Nebuchadnezzar takes the most valuable temple vessels back to Babylonia for use in the service of his god Marduk.

3. Next, Nebuchadnezzar orders Ashpenaz, one of his officers, to take hostages from Judah's royal house and Judah's first families.

4. They are youths who are handsome, intelligent, have a good understanding of various subjects, and can learn Aramaic literature and language.

5. These hostages are given royal treatment from Nebuchadnezzar. This treatment means that they will receive their meals directly from the King's table, which includes everything he eats. His master plan is to provide training and a menu for three years, and then examine them to see if they are fit to serve.

6. Now among these were of the children of Judah, Daniel, Hananiah, Mishael, and Azariah:
7. Unto whom the prince of the eunuchs gave names: for he gave unto Daniel *the name* of Belteshazzar; and to Hananiah, of Shadrach; and to Mishael, of Meshach; and to Azariah, of Abednego.
8. But Daniel purposed in his heart that he would not defile himself with the portion of the king's meat, nor with the wine which he drank: therefore he requested of the prince of the eunuchs that he might not defile himself.
9. Now God had brought Daniel into favour and tender love with the prince of the eunuchs.
10. And the prince of the eunuchs said unto Daniel, I fear my lord the king, who hath appointed your meat and your drink: for why should he see your faces worse liking than the children which *are* of your sort? then shall ye make *me* endanger my head to the king.

6. **Among these** - This expression reveals that there were other young men selected for the same training. **Daniel** - Meaning, "God is my judge." **Hananiah** - Meaning, "Yahweh is gracious." **Mishael** - Meaning, "Who belongs to God?" **Azariah** - Meaning, "Yahweh helps."
7. **Belteshazzar** - Likely meaning, "Bel protect his [the king's] life." **Shadrach** - A satisfactory explanation as to the origin of this name has not yet been found as it doesn't appear to be Babylonian. **Meshach** - A satisfactory explanation as to the origin of this name has not yet been found as it doesn't appear to be Babylonian. **Abednego** - It's generally agreed that this name stands for *'Eded-Nebo*, "servant of [the god] Nabu."
8. **Not defile himself** - It appears Daniel and the three Hebrews boys did not want to do anything that would jeopardize their physical, mental, and spiritual development.
10. **Endanger my head** - Literal translation is, "Ye make my head punishable with the king." The chief eunuch was held responsible for the physical state of those who were put under his charge.

EG White Notes

Perceiving the superior talents of these youthful captives, King Nebuchadnezzar determined to prepare them to fill important positions in his kingdom. That they might be fully qualified for their life at court, according to Oriental custom, they were to be taught the language of the Chaldeans, and to be subjected for three years to a thorough course of physical and intellectual discipline. *FE 77*

The meat served on the kings table was often portions of the sacrifices offered in heathen temples, and the wine too was dedicated to the gods, a portion being poured out as a libation before the beginning of each meal. All who partook of the yields thus dedicated to the gods, were regarded as connected with the heathen worship. Moreover, many articles of food, such as swine's flesh and things of an abominable character, were by the law given to Israel forbidden as unfit for food. *Ms 2b, 1895*

The Clear and Present Paraphrase

6. Among the hostages taken from the royal house of Judah are Daniel Hananiah, Mishael, and Azariah.
7. Daniel Hananiah, Mishael, and Azariah pass the examination and are selected to serve in the king's court. The young men are then castrated and assigned new names by Ashpenaz, who is in charge of all eunuchs. Accordingly, Daniel's name is changed to Belteshazzar; Hananiah is now called Shadrach, Mishael will be called Meshach, and Azariah will be known as Abed-nego.
8. Daniel decides he will not dishonor God by consuming the king's food and drinks that have been offered to idols. Therefore, the Hebrew asks for permission to abstain from any food or drinks that would defile him.
9. God had brought Daniel into favor and compassion with Ashpenaz
10. However, after the prince of the eunuchs hears Daniel's request, he says, "I am scared because the king has provided specific food and drinks for you guys, and once he notices how anemic you'll look, compared to all the others, he will hold me responsible."

11. Then said Daniel to Melzar, whom the prince of the eunuchs had set over Daniel, Hananiah, Mishael, and Azariah,
12. Prove thy servants, I beseech thee, ten days; and let them give us pulse to eat, and water to drink.
13. Then let our countenances be looked upon before thee, and the countenance of the children that eat of the portion of the king's meat: and as thou seest, deal with thy servants.
14. So he consented to them in this matter, and proved them ten days.
15. And at the end of ten days their countenances appeared fairer and fatter in flesh than all the children which did eat the portion of the king's meat.
16. Thus Melzar took away the portion of their meat, and the wine that they should drink; and gave them pulse.

11. **Melzar** - It is believed Melzar was Daniel's immediate tutor.
12. **Ten days** - This seems a short period of time to produce any noticeable change in their appearance, but divine power was united with human effort. **Pulse** - Food that is derived from plants.
13. **Countenance** - Appearance
15. **Fairer and fatter** - At the end of the allotted time, the Hebrew's appearance was visibly healthier and stronger.
16. **Took away** - To lift, bear up, carry, take

EG White Notes

In reaching this decision, the Hebrew youth did not act presumptuously but in firm reliance upon God. They did not choose to be singular, but they would be so rather than dishonor God. Should they compromise with wrong in this instance by yielding to the pressure of circumstances, their departure from principle would weaken their sense of right and their abhorrence of wrong. The first wrong step would lead to others, until, their connection with Heaven severed, they would be swept away by temptation. *PK 483*

God brought Daniel into favor with the prince of the eunuchs because he behaved himself. He kept before him the fear of the Lord. His companions never saw in his life anything that would lead them astray. Those who had charge over him loved him, because he carried with him the fragrance of a Christlike disposition. *The Upward Look p.47*

The Clear and Present Paraphrase

11. Daniel then pays a visit to Melzar, the personal tutor to the three Hebrew boys, and says to him,
12. "Put us to the test for ten days; give us only vegetables to eat and water to drink.
13. Then compare our appearance against those who are eating the king's food, and then make a decision according to the results."
14. Melzar listens intently to Daniel and agrees to this ten-day test.
15. At the end of ten days, it's apparent that Daniel and the three Hebrew boys are healthier than all the others who were eating the king's food.
16. So Melzar allows them to stay on this diet and eliminates the king's food so that they will no longer be forced to eat from his table.

17. As for these four children, God gave them knowledge and skill in all learning and wisdom: and Daniel had understanding in all visions and dreams.
18. Now at the end of the days that the king had said he should bring them in, then the prince of the eunuchs brought them in before Nebuchadnezzar.
19. And the king communed with them; and among them all was found none like Daniel, Hananiah, Mishael, and Azariah: therefore stood they before the king.
20. And in all matters of wisdom *and* understanding, that the king enquired of them, he found them ten times better than all the magicians *and* astrologers that *were* in all his realm.
21. And Daniel continued *even* unto the first year of king Cyrus.

17. **Visions and dreams** - Daniel's friends all had the same capabilities; however, it appears that Daniel was chosen as God's special messenger.
18. **At the end of days** - This was the end of the three years, which consisted of 1) The year the Hebrew captives arrived in Babylon. 2) King Nebuchadnezzar's full-year one. 3) Nebuchadnezzar's full-year two, in which Daniel and his friends "stood before the king.
19. **Communed with them** - This was the end of the training period, and now the chief eunuch presented his graduates to the king for examination. **Stood they before the king** - They were now part of the King's royal service (see chapter 2:2)
20. **Magicians** - Divination, magic, exorcism, and astrology was a common practice.
21. **Unto the first year** - Some commentators believe this verse implies Daniel did not live beyond Cyrus' first year, which contradicts Dan 10:1. However, the text is not suggesting Daniel died in the first year of the Persian ruler, but rather this chapter was likely written during the first year of his reign.

EG White Notes

At the end of the ten days' trial the result was found to be the opposite of the prince's fears. "Their countenances appeared fairer and fatter in flesh than all the children which did eat the portion of the king's meat." In personal appearance the Hebrew youth showed a marked superiority over their companions. As a result, Daniel and his associates were permitted to continue their simple diet during their entire course of training. *PK 484*

When the time came for the youth in training to be tested, the Hebrews were examined, with other candidates, for the service of the kingdom. But "among them all was found none like Daniel, Hananiah, Mishael, and Azariah." Their keen comprehension, their wide knowledge, their choice and exact language, testified to the unimpaired strength and vigor of their mental powers. "In all matters of wisdom and understanding, that the king inquired of them, he found them ten times better than all the magicians and astrologers that were in all his realm;" "therefore stood they before the king." *PK 485*

The Clear and Present Paraphrase

17. So God blesses Daniel and the three Hebrew boys with wisdom and skill in practically everything they did. To Daniel, God not only blesses him with wisdom and skill, but he also blesses Daniel with the ability to interpret visions and dreams.

18. At the end of their three-year training, Ashpenaz takes Daniel and the three Hebrew boys to be examined by Nebuchadnezzar.

19. As the king examines them, he soon discovers that Daniel, Hananiah, Mishael, and Azariah are far more advanced than all the others. So the king decides to make all four of them permanent members of his court.

20. Soon Nebuchadnezzar will discover that, regardless of the issue or problem, Daniel and his friends are far more superior in solving them than any magician or psychic in Babylon.

21. Daniel continues to serve in the royal court, even after Babylon is conquered by Cyrus.

DANIEL 1 - TEST YOUR KNOWLEDGE

1. What were the original names of the three Hebrew boys? *(p.19)* _____

2. Who was the Master of the eunuchs? *(p.16)* _____

3. Why did God give Daniel favor with the prince of the eunuchs? *(p.21)* _____
   _____

4. What is the meaning of Daniel's name? *(p. 16)* _____
   _____

5. Who was the king of Judah when Nebuchadnezzar besieged it? *(p.18)* _____
   _____

6. True or False - The only issue with the king's meat is that it was unclean. *(p. 19)*

7. What is pulse? *(p. 20)* _____

8. Who was the chief god of the Babylonians? *(p. 16)* _____

9. How many days was Daniel given to prove his diet was superior to the king's diet? *(p.20)* _____

10. What was Daniel's Babylonian name? *(p. 18)* _____

Questions for Discussion:

1. Do our diets make a difference in our mindsets?

2. Does healthful living only consist of what we eat, or are there other factors involved?

King Nebuchadnezzar has a dream, but it's not an ordinary dream. This dream is a special message from God directly to the king. However, this message is not only for Nebuchadnezzar, it's for the entire world.

Daniel 2

The Image of the Past, Present, and Future

CHAPTER 2

1. And in the second year of the reign of Nebuchadnezzar Nebuchadnezzar dreamed dreams, wherewith his spirit was troubled, and his sleep brake from him.
2. Then the king commanded to call the magicians, and the astrologers, and the sorcerers, and the Chaldeans, for to shew the king his dreams. So they came and stood before the king.
3. And the king said unto them, I have dreamed a dream, and my spirit was troubled to know the dream.
4. Then spake the Chaldeans to the king in Syriack, O king, live for ever: tell thy servants the dream, and we will shew the interpretation.
5. The king answered and said to the Chaldeans, The thing is gone from me: if ye will not make known unto me the dream, with the interpretation thereof, ye shall be cut in pieces, and your houses shall be made a dunghill.

CHAPTER 2

1. **Dreamed dreams** - Possibly used in the plural sense to describe the series of incidents in his dreams. **Was troubled** - The dream that Nebuchadnezzar experienced clearly had a strong impression upon him.
2. **Sorcerers** - "to use enchantments."
3. **To know the dream** - Some have suggested that the king knew the dream but was just testing the wise men, but the king appears too concerned about the meaning of the dream to the point he was willing to put them all to death.
4. **Syriack** - "Aramaic" The royal family and the ruling class of the empire were Aramaic-speaking Chaldeans.
5. **The thing is gone from me** - "has gone." Nebuchadnezzar clearly was not able to recall the particulars of the dream. **Dunghill** - Some interpret this clause as meaning their houses would be turned into public restrooms. The LXX which is the earliest extant Greek translation of the Old Testament from the original Hebrew reads, "your houses shall be spoiled."

EG White Notes

CHAPTER 2

A most interesting and important history is given in Daniel 2. Nebuchadnezzar, king of Babylon, dreamed a dream which he could not bring to his remembrance when he awoke. "Then the king commanded to call the magicians, and the astrologers, and the sorcerers, and the Chaldeans," those whom he had exalted and upon whom he depended, and, relating the circumstances, demanded that they should tell him the dream. The wise men stood before the king in terror; for they had no ray of light in regard to his dream. They could only say, "O king, live forever: tell thy servants the dream, and we will show the interpretation." "The king answered and said to the Chaldeans, The thing is gone from me: if ye will not make known unto me the dream with the interpretation thereof, ye shall be cut in pieces, and your houses made a dunghill." *FE 410*

The Clear and Present Paraphrase

CHAPTER 2

1. Two years after Nebuchadnezzar's inaugural year, Nebuchadnezzar has a dream that really troubles him. As a matter of fact, this dream troubles him so much that he can no longer sleep.

2. So he calls all his established fortune tellers, astrologers, scientists, and priests and asks them to explain to him his dream.

3. He says to them, "I had a dream last night that really bothered me, and I need you guys to tell me what my dream meant."

4. The Chaldeans respond to Nebuchadnezzar in his native tongue and say, "May the gods give long days and everlasting years to the king, my Lord. Describe your dream to us, and we will tell you its meaning."

5. Nebuchadnezzar replies, "I can't remember what my dream was about, but I know that I had a dream, so listen, and listen good. If you guys can't tell me what my dream was and give me the meaning of my dream, I will slice each and every one of you limb from limb and turn your homes into public waste dumps.

6. But if ye shew the dream, and the interpretation thereof, ye shall receive of me gifts and rewards and great honour: therefore shew me the dream, and the interpretation thereof.
7. They answered again and said, Let the king tell his servants the dream, and we will shew the interpretation of it.
8. The king answered and said, I know of certainty that ye would gain the time, because ye see the thing is gone from me.
9. But if ye will not make known unto me the dream, *there is but* one decree for you: for ye have prepared lying and corrupt words to speak before me, till the time be changed: therefore tell me the dream, and I shall know that ye can shew me the interpretation thereof.
10. The Chaldeans answered before the king, and said, There is not a man upon the earth that can shew the king's matter: therefore *there is* no king, lord, nor ruler, *that* asked such things at any magician, or astrologer, or Chaldean.

8. **Gain the time** - Literally, "Buy time."
9. **One decree for you** - Literally, "your law is one." The word for "decree" may also be rendered "sentence" or "penalty." **Time be changed** - Either until the king should forget the whole situation or until they could craft a reply.
10. **Not a man** - The Chaldeans were compelled to admit their inability to reveal the king's dream.

EG White Notes

But if ye show the dream, and the interpretation thereof, ye shall receive of me gifts and rewards and great honor: therefore show me the dream, and the interpretation thereof." Still the wise men returned the same answer, "Let the king tell his servants the dream, and we will show the interpretation of it."

Nebuchadnezzar began to see that the men whom he trusted to reveal mysteries through their boasted wisdom, failed him in his great perplexity, and he said, "I know of certainty that ye would gain the time, because ye see the thing is gone from me. *FE 410*

The Clear and Present Paraphrase

6. On the other hand, if you can tell me what I dreamed and give me the explanation of the dream, I will provide you with gifts and rewards, so tell me my dream and its meaning now!"

7. "Your Majesty," they reply, "if you would just tell us what you dreamed, we know we can provide you the meaning of that dream."

8. Nebuchadnezzar responds, "I clearly see that you guys are stalling for time. You think because I can't remember my dream, I'll eventually forget about this whole situation.

9. Well, listen closely; if you don't tell me what I dreamed, there is only one outcome for you because I know what you guys are trying to do. You'll try to make something up, hoping that by the time you tell me, I would've forgotten the dream. So tell me what I dreamed, and if you can tell me this, then I'll know that you can tell me the meaning as well."

10. The men try to reason with the king, "Your Majesty, no one can do this; and no man of power or authority that demands such a thing from his priests, fortune-tellers, and astrologers.

11. And *it is* a rare thing that the king requireth, and there is none other that can shew it before the king, except the gods, whose dwelling is not with flesh.

12. For this cause the king was angry and very furious, and commanded to destroy all the wise *men* of Babylon.

13. And the decree went forth that the wise *men* should be slain; and they sought Daniel and his fellows to be slain.

14. Then Daniel answered with counsel and wisdom to Arioch the captain of the king's guard, which was gone forth to slay the wise *men* of Babylon:

15. He answered and said to Arioch the king's captain, Why *is* the decree *so* hasty from the king? Then Arioch made the thing known to Daniel.

16. Then Daniel went in, and desired of the king that he would give him time, and that he would shew the king the interpretation.

11. **Rare** - "difficult." **The gods** - Some suggest that these wise men were claiming to be in contact with low-level deities, but the higher gods were unapproachable.

12. **Commanded to destroy** - This was bold of the king due to the fact that the men were the learned classes of society.

13. **They sought Daniel** - Even though Daniel and his friends were part of the profession of "wise men," the fact that they were recent graduates is a sufficient explanation of why they weren't part of the initial call to interpret the dream. The King appeared to only call the established "wise men" at that time to interpret his dream.

14. **Wisdom** - In Aramaic, this is also translated as "taste" or "discretion."

15. **Hasty** - The LXX has *pikros*, which means "bitter" or "harsh." Some insist that the original meaning has the basic idea of urgency.

16. **Give him time** - Nebuchadnezzar's previous contact with Daniel left a favorable impression upon the king, which may have opened the door to Daniel getting this opportunity.

EG White Notes

Then was the king "angry and very furious, and commanded to destroy all the wise men of Babylon." *FE 410-411*

Among those sought for by the officers who were preparing to fulfill the provisions of the royal decree, were Daniel and his friends. When told that according to the decree they also must die, "with counsel and wisdom" Daniel inquired of Arioch, the captain of the king's guard, "Why is the decree so hasty from the king?" Arioch told him the story of the king's perplexity over his remarkable dream, and of his failure to secure help from those in whom he had hitherto placed fullest confidence. Upon hearing this, Daniel, taking his life in his hands, ventured into the king's presence and begged that time be granted, that he might petition his God to reveal to him the dream and its interpretation. *PK 493*

The Clear and Present Paraphrase

11. Please understand this is extremely difficult, and the only way that your dream can be known is if the supreme gods in heaven reveal it, but those gods don't talk to men."

12. At this point, Nebuchadnezzar goes into a rage and orders the execution of every wise man in Babylon.

13. So the orders are drawn up that every wise man is to be executed, and officers arrive to carry this out on Daniel and his friends.

14. Arioch, commander of the king's guard, finds Daniel and confronts him with the king's order; however, Daniel responds in wisdom and tact.

15. Once Daniel understands the king's order, he asks Arioch, "Why would a harsh order like this come from the king so urgently?" Then Arioch explains the whole story to Daniel.

16. After understanding the situation, Daniel requests permission to stand before the king to ask for a 24-hour extension. Daniel promises that by tomorrow he will know the dream and will be able to give him the interpretation as well.

KJV Bible

17. Then Daniel went to his house, and made the thing known to Hananiah, Mishael, and Azariah, his companions:
18. That they would desire mercies of the God of heaven concerning this secret; that Daniel and his fellows should not perish with the rest of the wise *men* of Babylon.
19. Then was the secret revealed unto Daniel in a night vision. Then Daniel blessed the God of heaven.
20. Daniel answered and said, Blessed be the name of God for ever and ever: for wisdom and might are his:
21. And he changeth the times and the seasons: he removeth kings, and setteth up kings: he giveth wisdom unto the wise, and knowledge to them that know understanding:
22. He revealeth the deep and secret things: he knoweth what *is* in the darkness, and the light dwelleth with him.

Daniel Commentary

18. **Desire mercies** - Daniel and his three friends were able to approach God with faith and confidence because they lived up to His revealed will to the best of their knowledge and ability.
19. **Night Vision** - Something seen. **Daniel blessed** - Once Daniel received the divine revelation, his first thought was to praise the Revealer of secrets.
20. **Name of God** - This expression is frequently used to refer to the being, power, and important activity of God. "Name" is often used in the Bible synonymously with "character."
21. **And he** - Better translated, "It is he that changeth," etc. **Times and the seasons** - These two words are almost identical. Seasons may refer to a more specific point of time; Times seems to refer to a period of time.
22. **Deep** - The things we, as humans, are unable to comprehend until revealed. **Darkness** - That which man is unable to see is seen clearly by God.

EG White Notes	The Clear and Present Paraphrase

To this request the monarch acceded. "Then Daniel went to his house, and made the thing known to Hananiah, Mishael, and Azariah, his companions." Together they sought for wisdom from the Source of light and knowledge. Their faith was strong in the consciousness that God had placed them where they were, that they were doing His work and meeting the demands of duty. In times of perplexity and danger they had always turned to Him for guidance and protection, and He had proved an ever-present help. Now with contrition of heart they submitted themselves anew to the Judge of the earth, pleading that He would grant them deliverance in this their time of special need. And they did not plead in vain. The God whom they had honored, now honored them. The Spirit of the Lord rested upon them, and to Daniel, "in a night vision," was revealed the king's dream and its meaning. *PK 493-494*

Daniel's first act was to thank God for the revelation given him. "Blessed be the name of God forever and ever..." *PK 494*

17. King Nebuchadnezzar listens to Daniel's proposal and agrees to its terms. Daniel quickly goes home and shares everything with Hananiah, Mishael, and Azariah.

18. Daniel tells them that they must pray for mercy from the God of heaven to show them the dream and the interpretation so they are not executed with the other wise men of Babylon.

19. That night, God reveals to Daniel the exact dream He had previously given to Nebuchadnezzar. Daniel, filled with joy and thanksgiving, praises the God of heaven.

20. As he's praising God, Daniel says, "Praise God forever and ever! All wisdom and power are His!

21. Times and Seasons are not regulated by happenstance or coincidence; it is God who controls these things. It is He who removes kings and sets up kings. He is the One who gives wisdom to those we call wise and knowledge to those we call intelligent!

22. It is He who reveals mysteries that no one else has the capability to know. He knows what's in the darkness because the light shines from Him.

23. I thank thee, and praise thee, O thou God of my fathers, who hast given me wisdom and might, and hast made known unto me now what we desired of thee: for thou hast *now* made known unto us the king's matter.
24. Therefore Daniel went in unto Arioch, whom the king had ordained to destroy the wise *men* of Babylon: he went and said thus unto him; Destroy not the wise *men* of Babylon: bring me in before the king, and I will shew unto the king the interpretation.
25. Then Arioch brought in Daniel before the king in haste, and said thus unto him, I have found a man of the captives of Judah, that will make known unto the king the interpretation.
26. The king answered and said to Daniel, whose name *was* Belteshazzar, Art thou able to make known unto me the dream which I have seen, and the interpretation thereof?

23. **Thank thee** - May be translated as: "To thee, O God of my fathers, I give thanks."
24. **Destroy not the wise men** - Scriptures tell us that the righteous are "the salt of the earth." Salt is a preserver. Daniel became "salt" to the wise men as he "preserved" their lives.
25. **In haste** - Most likely, this was due to his great joy that the secret had been discovered. **I have found** - The construction of Arioch's statement would be the natural way of announcing the discovery even though it appears he takes undeserved credit for himself.
26. **Belteshazzar** - In the king's presence, Daniel naturally assumed his Babylonian name.

EG White Notes

Going immediately to Arioch, whom the king had commanded to destroy the wise men, Daniel said, "Destroy not the wise men of Babylon: bring me in before the king, and I will show unto the king the interpretation." Quickly the officer ushered Daniel in before the king, with the words, "I have found a man of the captives of Judah, that will make known unto the king the interpretation." *PK 494*

Behold the Jewish captive, calm and self-possessed, in the presence of the monarch of the world's most powerful empire. In his first words he disclaimed honor for himself and exalted God as the source of all wisdom. To the anxious inquiry of the king, "Art thou able to make known unto me the dream which I have seen, and the interpretation thereof?" *PK 494*

The Clear and Present Paraphrase

23. I thank You and praise You, Oh God of my fathers! I thank You and praise Your holy name because what we asked, You have revealed to me. You have blessed us to know the king's dream!"

24. Immediately, Daniel goes to see Arioch, who is also in charge of carrying out the king's orders to execute Babylon's wise men. Daniel says to Arioch, "You won't have to execute the wise men of Babylon. Take me to the king, I know what he dreamed, and I can also tell him what it means."

25. Arioch rushes Daniel to the king and says to the king, "Your Majesty, I have found someone among the Jewish captives who claims he can tell the king his dream and interpret it for him."

26. "Daniel," begins Nebuchadnezzar, "Do you think you can tell me my dream and what it means?"

27. Daniel answered in the presence of the king, and said, The secret which the king hath demanded cannot the wise *men*, the astrologers, the magicians, the soothsayers, shew unto the king;
28. But there is a God in heaven that revealeth secrets, and maketh known to the king Nebuchadnezzar what shall be in the latter days. Thy dream, and the visions of thy head upon thy bed, are these;
29. As for thee, O king, thy thoughts came *into thy mind* upon thy bed, what should come to pass hereafter: and he that revealeth secrets maketh known to thee what shall come to pass.
30. But as for me, this secret is not revealed to me for *any* wisdom that I have more than any living, but for *their* sakes that shall make known the interpretation to the king, and that thou mightest know the thoughts of thy heart.

27. **Cannot the wise men** - Daniel didn't have a desire to exalt himself above the wise men; however, he hoped to turn the king's eyes to the God of heaven. **The astrologers, the magicians** - (see chapter 1:20) **Soothsayers** - The generally accepted meaning is "the deciders," or "the determiners [of destiny]." From the position of the stars, soothsayers believed they could tell the future.
28. **Latter days** - Future days
29. **Hereafter** - The prophecy started in Nebuchadnezzar's day but carries us all the way to the Second Coming and the end of the world.
30. **Their sakes** - The clause reads literally, "but on account of the thing that they may make known to the king the interpretation." The LXX provides this meaning, "Moreover, this mystery has not been revealed to me by reason of wisdom which is in me beyond all living, but for the sake of making known the interpretation to the king, that thou mightest know the thoughts of thine heart."

EG White Notes

"The secret which the king hath demanded cannot the wise men, the astrologers, the magicians, the soothsayers, show unto the king; but there is a God in heaven that revealeth secrets, and maketh known to the king Nebuchadnezzar what shall be in the latter days." *PK 494*

"Thy dream," Daniel declared, "and the visions of thy head upon thy bed, are these; As for thee, O king, thy thoughts came into thy mind upon thy bed, what should come to pass hereafter: and He that revealeth secrets maketh known to thee what shall come to pass. But as for me, this secret is not revealed to me for any wisdom that I have more than any living, but for their sakes that shall make known the interpretation to the king, and that thou mightest know the thoughts of thy heart." *PK 497*

The Clear and Present Paraphrase

27. "Your Majesty," Daniel responds, "I just want to say that there is no philosopher, astrologer, or fortune-teller living on this planet that can do what you're asking.

28. However, there is a God in heaven who can reveal and explain all mysteries. As a matter of fact, it was this same God who gave you this dream in order for you to know what will happen in the future. So let me tell you the dream you had while you were sleeping:

29. Now, before you went to sleep that night, you were sitting on the edge of your bed, wondering what will happen to your kingdom in the future; And the God of heaven actually revealed it to you!

30. I know this, not because I'm more intelligent than everyone, but God revealed your same dream to me to save the lives of your advisors and because He wanted you to know what will happen to your kingdom.

KJV Bible

31. Thou, O king, sawest, and behold a great image. This great image, whose brightness *was* excellent, stood before thee; and the form thereof *was* terrible.
32. This image's head *was* of fine gold, his breast and his arms of silver, his belly and his thighs of brass,
33. His legs of iron, his feet part of iron and part of clay.
34. Thou sawest till that a stone was cut out without hands, which smote the image upon his feet *that were* of iron and clay, and brake them to pieces.
35. Then was the iron, the clay, the brass, the silver, and the gold, broken to pieces together, and became like the chaff of the summer threshingfloors; and the wind carried them away, that no place was found for them: and the stone that smote the image became a great mountain, and filled the whole earth.

Daniel Commentary

31. **Image** - In Aramaic, "a statue." **Whose brightness was excellent** - As the LXX states, "whose appearance was extraordinary." **Terrible** - Dreadful.
32. **Fine gold** - That is, "pure gold." **Brass** - Rather, "bronze," or "copper."
33. **Legs** - The word that is translated here appears to refer to the lower part of the legs. The word translated "thighs" (vs. 32) refers to the upper part of the hips. Precisely where on the leg the transition from brass to iron occurred is not clear from these words. **Clay** - It seems a better translation of this would be "molded clay" or "earthenware" rather than merely "clay."
34. **Cut out** - "Broken out." **Without hands** - Without the help of human activity.
35. **Chaff** - For a description of threshing as carried out in ancient Oriental lands, see Ruth 3:2; Matt 3:12. Inspiration has attached no particular significance to the "chaff" and the "wind" that blows it away; therefore, it's best to consider them as details added to make a complete picture.

EG White Notes

"Thou, O king, sawest, and behold a great image. This great image, whose brightness was excellent, stood before thee; and the form thereof was terrible. This image's head was of fine gold, his breast and his arms of silver, his belly and his thighs of brass, his legs of iron, his feet part of iron and part of clay. *PK 497*

"Thou sawest till that a stone was cut out without hands, which smote the image upon his feet that were of iron and clay, and brake them to pieces. Then was the iron, the clay, the brass, the silver, and the gold, broken to pieces together, and became like the chaff of the summer threshing floors; and the wind carried them away, that no place was found for them: and the stone that smote the image became a great mountain, and filled the whole earth. *PK 497*

The Clear and Present Paraphrase

31. In your dream, you saw an enormous statue of a man. The statue seemed to be glowing with light all around it, and it was very frightening to see.
32. The head of this statue was made of pure gold, its chest and arms were made of silver, its waist and hips were made of bronze.
33. Its legs were made of iron, and its feet were made partly of iron and partly of molded clay.
34. Now, while you were observing this statue, a huge boulder broke off a mountain without anyone touching it; this boulder was propelled with great force towards this statue striking its feet of iron and clay, and the impact caused the feet to immediately crumble into pieces.
35. When the feet crumbled, the rest of the statue collapsed and broke into fine particles similar to the particles of grain left over when they are separated from the plant. Then a strong wind came and blew the dust away, and there was no trace of the metals left over. And finally, you watched the boulder get bigger and bigger until it became a mountain that filled the whole earth.

KJV Bible	Daniel Commentary
36. This *is* the dream; and we will tell the interpretation thereof before the king.	**36. We will tell** - The plural may indicate that Daniel classified his companions with himself, in which Daniel may have wished to acknowledge their part in the matter (vs. 17,18).
37. Thou, O king, *art* a king of kings: for the God of heaven hath given thee a kingdom, power, and strength, and glory.	**37. A kingdom** - According to Genesis, the city of Babylon was part of the kingdom founded by Nimrod, the great-grandson of Noah. A number of city-states existed in the valleys of the Tigris and Euphrates early on, and through war and consolidation was taken over by multiple kings over the centuries. Eventually, Babylon's territory came under rule by the Chaldeans in which Nabopolassar (reigned 626-605 BC) was the founder. The city had its golden age under the reign of Nebuchadnezzar (605-562 BC), which lasted until the Medes and Persians conquered the city in 539 BC
38. And wheresoever the children of men dwell, the beasts of the field and the fowls of the heaven hath he given into thine hand, and hath made thee ruler over them all. Thou *art* this head of gold.	**38. Thou art this head** - Nebuchadnezzar was the Neo-Babylon Empire personified. **Gold** - An abundance of gold was used to beautify Babylon. The prophet Jeremiah compares Babylon to a golden cup (Jer 51:7).

EG White Notes

"This is the dream," confidently declared Daniel; and the king, listening with closest attention to every particular, knew it was the very dream over which he had been so troubled. Thus his mind was prepared to receive with favor the interpretation. The King of kings was about to communicate great truth to the Babylonian monarch. God would reveal that He has power over the kingdoms of the world, power to enthrone and to dethrone kings. Nebuchadnezzar's mind was to be awakened, if possible, to a sense of his responsibility to Heaven. The events of the future, reaching down to the end of time, were to be opened before him. *PK 497-498*

Had the rulers of Babylon--that richest of all earthly kingdoms--kept always before them the fear of Jehovah, they would have been given wisdom and power which would have bound them to Him and kept them strong. But they made God their refuge only when harassed and perplexed. *PK 501*

The Clear and Present Paraphrase

36. That is what you saw in your dream, and here is what it all means:

37. You are the greatest king among earthly kings. It is the God of heaven that has given you this Kingdom of Babylon, and has given you power, might, and glory,

38. Not only that, but He has given you rulership over people, animals, and birds; so the golden head on that statue represents you and your kingdom.

KJV Bible	Daniel Commentary

39. And after thee shall arise another kingdom inferior to thee, and another third kingdom of brass, which shall bear rule over all the earth.

40. And the fourth kingdom shall be strong as iron: forasmuch as iron breaketh in pieces and subdueth all things: and as iron that breaketh all these, shall it break in pieces and bruise.

41. And whereas thou sawest the feet and toes, part of potters' clay, and part of iron, the kingdom shall be divided; but there shall be in it of the strength of the iron, forasmuch as thou sawest the iron mixed with miry clay.

39. Another kingdom inferior - As silver is inferior to gold, the Medo-Persian Empire was inferior to the Neo-Babylonian Empire in luxury and magnificence. This second kingdom was often called Medo-Persia because it began as a combination of Media and Persia. **Third kingdom** - The successor of Medo-Persia was the Greek Empire. The Hebrew word for Greece is Yawan (Javan) which is a son of Japheth and is mentioned immediately after Madai, the father of the Medes (see Gen 10:2). **Rule over all the earth** - Greece's dominion was not literally over the whole world, but it stood above all the other empires, and none were equal to it.

40. Fourth kingdom - Rome is the kingdom that dominated the world after Greece.

41. Feet - Likely the United States of America as this power is the third and final phase of Babylon. **Toes** - Presumably ten. These ten toes correlate with the ten horns in chapter 7, and have shown to be the ten kingships that preceeded Rome and return as the Kings of the East (see Rev 16:12). **Miry clay** - This represents the Papacy.

EG White Notes

In the history of nations the student of God's word may behold the literal fulfillment of divine prophecy. Babylon, shattered and broken at last, passed away because in prosperity its rulers had regarded themselves as independent of God, and had ascribed the glory of their kingdom to human achievement. The Medo-Persian realm was visited by the wrath of Heaven because in it God's law had been trampled underfoot. The fear of the Lord had found no place in the hearts of the vast majority of the people. Wickedness, blasphemy, and corruption prevailed. The kingdoms that followed were even more base and corrupt; and these sank lower and still lower in the scale of moral worth. *PK 501-502*

The mingling of church craft and state craft is represented by the iron and the clay. This union is weakening all the power of the churches. This investing in the church with the power of the state will bring evil results. *1MR 51*

The Clear and Present Paraphrase

39. But after some time passes, the Medes and Persians will conquer Babylon. Now even though they will conquer this kingdom, Medo-Persia will be inferior to Babylon in glory and moral values, just as silver is inferior to gold. Then that kingdom will be replaced by Greece, which is represented by bronze, but that kingdom will be even more inferior in glory and moral values than the Medes and Persians—while at the same time ruling a larger part of the world.

40. Then Rome will come into power. This kingdom will be as strong as iron. And just as iron can crush all other metals, Rome will crush every kingdom that stands in its way. However, this kingdom will be even more inferior in glory and moral values than all the kingdoms that preceded it.

41. And as you saw the feet and toes that were partly clay and partly iron, you must understand that in the last days, the continuation of iron Rome, known as Protestant America, and the ten Kings of the East, will be allied with the Papacy. In this manner, the Roman iron and Papal clay will be joined together.

KJV Bible

42. And *as* the toes of the feet *were* part of iron, and part of clay, *so* the kingdom shall be partly strong, and partly broken.
43. And whereas thou sawest iron mixed with miry clay, they shall mingle themselves with the seed of men: but they shall not cleave one to another, even as iron is not mixed with clay.
44. And in the days of these kings shall the God of heaven set up a kingdom, which shall never be destroyed: and the kingdom shall not be left to other people, *but* it shall break in pieces and consume all these kingdoms, and it shall stand for ever.

Daniel Commentary

42. **Toes** - Likely a reference to the kings of this world, who were once part of the Roman Empire and will become part of an end-time coalition with the Papacy. **Kingdom** - An in-depth study of Bible prophecy reveals that the United States of America is prophetically the continuation of the Roman Empire. Therefore, the Protestant superpower is most likely represented as the feet of iron, which also mingles with the Papal clay before the end of the world. **Broken** - "Fragile" or "brittle."
43. **With the seed of men** - This phrase may refer to the people of the world who are enticed to join the Papal-Protestant union. **Shall not cleave** - may refer to the fact that the alliance between America, the Papacy, and the kingdoms of this world ultimately loses its adhesiveness.
44. **Days of these kings** - This prophecy occurs while these kingdoms are at the height of their powers. **Set up a kingdom** - The Kingdom of God would ultimately succeed the iron and clay phase (see Revelation 21:2).

EG White Notes

The image revealed to Nebuchadnezzar, while representing the deterioration of the kingdoms of the earth in power and glory, also fitly represents the deterioration of religion and morality among the people of these kingdoms. As nations forget God, in like proportion they become weak morally. *4BC 1168*

We have come to a time when God's sacred work is represented by the feet of the image in which the iron was mixed with the miry clay. *1MR 51*

...statesmen will uphold the spurious sabbath, and will mingle their religious faith with the observance of this child of the papacy, placing it above the Sabbath which the Lord has sanctified and blessed, setting it apart for man to keep holy, as a sign between Him and His people to a thousand generations." *1MR 51*

The Clear and Present Paraphrase

42. And as the toes on the feet were partly iron and partly clay, the union that the kings of this world will establish with Protestant America and the Papacy will be partly strong and partly fragile.

43. Just as you saw the iron mixed with clay, Protestant America will attempt to bind this worldwide union together with Papal ideology. However, just as clay won't stick to iron, neither will this union hold together.

44. These nations will continue their quest to create a worldwide union right up until the time God comes and sets up the Kingdom of Christ. This Kingdom's reign will be established when Christ is seen coming in the clouds, which will bring an end to all other earthly kingdoms. Christ's Kingdom will never be conquered; it will stand forever.

KJV Bible

45. Forasmuch as thou sawest that the stone was cut out of the mountain without hands, and that it brake in pieces the iron, the brass, the clay, the silver, and the gold; the great God hath made known to the king what shall come to pass hereafter: and the dream *is* certain, and the interpretation thereof sure.
46. Then the king Nebuchadnezzar fell upon his face, and worshipped Daniel, and commanded that they should offer an oblation and sweet odours unto him.
47. The king answered unto Daniel, and said, Of a truth *it is*, that your God *is* a God of gods, and a Lord of kings, and a revealer of secrets, seeing thou couldest reveal this secret.
48. Then the king made Daniel a great man, and gave him many great gifts, and made him ruler over the whole province of Babylon, and chief of the governors over all the wise *men* of Babylon.
49. Then Daniel requested of the king, and he set Shadrach, Meshach, and Abed-nego, over the affairs of the province of Babylon: but Daniel *sat* in the gate of the king.

Daniel Commentary

45. **Stone** - A single stone, "used of slabs, stone vessels, or precious stones. The word "rock" is frequently used of God (Deut 32:4); however, there doesn't appear to be a connection, so it's apparent that the rock here is a literal rock and not symbolic of God.
46. **Fell upon his face** - This is a sign of respect and reverence. **Worshipped** - It's unlikely Daniel permitted worship (Rev 19:10). However, Daniel may have been directed not to interfere with the king at that moment. **Oblation** - Bloodless offering
47. **Your God is a God of gods** - The king now recognizes that Daniel's God is superior to any of his Babylonian gods.
48. **Chief of the governors** - Better, "chief prefect."
49. **Gate** - The place where Asian kings sat as judges and where chief councils convened (see Gen 19:1).

EG White Notes

Nebuchadnezzar felt that he could accept this interpretation as a divine revelation; for to Daniel had been revealed every detail of the dream. *4BC 1169*

Nebuchadnezzar revoked the decree for the destruction of the wise men. Their lives were spared because of Daniel's connection with the Revealer of secrets. *PK 499*

Daniel's exposition of the dream given by God to the king, resulted in his receiving honor and dignity. "The king Nebuchadnezzar fell upon his face, and worshiped Daniel, and commanded that they should offer an oblation and sweet odors unto him. The king answered unto Daniel, and said, Of a truth it is, that your God is a God of gods, and a Lord of kings, and a revealer of secrets, seeing thou couldest reveal this secret. *FCE 412*

The Clear and Present Paraphrase

45. And just as clear as you saw the stone, untouched, break loose from the mountain and shatter the iron, brass, clay, silver, and gold into pieces, you can be assured that everything you saw will happen because the dream is accurate and you can be confident in its interpretation."

46. Then Nebuchadnezzar falls on the ground and bows before Daniel out of sheer appreciation for him. He also orders incense and sacrifices to be made on Daniel's behalf.

47. The king then says to Daniel, "It is undeniable that your God is the greatest of all the gods because you were able to tell me what my dream was and the interpretation of it!"

48. Then the king lavishes Daniel with gifts and promotes him to be the ruler over the whole province of Babylon. He was also placed in authority over all the king's advisers.

49. Daniel then requests Shadrach, Meshach, and Abednego to be his assistants. Thus, his three friends become helpers with the affairs of the province, while Daniel takes care of the affairs of the city, working closely with the king.

Daniel 2 - Test your knowledge

1. Who did King Nebuchadnezzar call upon first in order to interpret his dream? *(p. 28)*_____

2. What did the king mean when he said, "I know of certainty that ye would gain the time?" *(p. 30)*_____

3. What was Daniel's first act after God revealed the interpretation of the king's dream to him? *(p. 35)*_____

4. Name all the elements of the image Nebuchadnezzar saw. *(p. 40)*_____
   _____

5. What hit the image and broke it into pieces? *(p. 40)*_____

6. Name each element of the image and its correlating nation. *(pp. 42-46)*_____
   _____
   _____
   _____

7. How does Ellen White further describe iron and clay? *(p. 47)*_____
   _____

8. True or False - Religion and morality deteriorated more and more with the succession of each world power. *(p. 47)*

9. According to Jeremiah 51:7, to what does God compare Babylon?_____
   _____

10. What part of the image pertains to the kings of the earth? *(p. 46)*_____

Questions for Discussion:

1. How do you think the United States of America fits into the image of Nebuchadnezzar's dream?

2. Do you think the astrologers, and soothsayers celebrated Daniel, or did they despise him? How can we relate to the relationship that Daniel had with the other wise men?

Shadrach, Meshach, and Abednego must decide if they will bow down to the golden image of Nebuchadnezzar or if they will stay true to Jehovah.

Daniel 3

The Fiery Trial of the Three Hebrews

CHAPTER 3

1. Nebuchadnezzar the king made an image of gold, whose height *was* threescore cubits, *and* the breadth thereof six cubits: he set it up in the plain of Dura, in the province of Babylon.
2. Then Nebuchadnezzar the king sent to gather together the princes, the governors, and the captains, the judges, the treasurers, the counsellors, the sheriffs, and all the rulers of the provinces, to come to the dedication of the image which Nebuchadnezzar the king had set up.
3. Then the princes, the governors, and captains, the judges, the treasurers, the counsellors, the sheriffs, and all the rulers of the provinces, were gathered together unto the dedication of the image that Nebuchadnezzar the king had set up; and they stood before the image that Nebuchadnezzar had set up.
4. Then an herald cried aloud, To you it is commanded, O people, nations, and languages,

CHAPTER 3

1. **Image of gold** - Nebuchadnezzar understood that only the head of gold, from the image in Daniel 2, represented Babylon. However, he was not satisfied that his kingdom was limited to the head of gold, so he created a head-to-toe golden image indicating Babylon's eternal glory. **Threescore cubits** - about 88 ft high by 9ft wide. Critics have pointed to the unusual proportions of the image as a reason to doubt this story's veracity. However, it was quite possible that the statue stood on a pedestal and was also included in the measurements.
2. **Princes** - In Persian times, this title designated officials at the head of satrapies, the largest division of the empire. **Governors** - "governors" or "prefects." **Judges** - Possibly "counselor" in Persian form. **Treasurers** - Origin has not been detected. **Counselors** - Aramaic "law bearer," or rather "judge," or possibly "adviser." **Sheriffs** - "police officer." **Rulers** - All lower officials of any importance.
4. **Herald** - "Messenger." This word is of Iranian origin.

CHAPTER 3 — EG White Notes

For a time afterward, Nebuchadnezzar was influenced by the fear of God; but his heart was not yet cleansed from worldly ambition and a desire for self-exaltation. The prosperity attending his reign filled him with pride. In time he ceased to honor God, and resumed his idol worship with increased zeal and bigotry. *PK 503*

The words, "Thou art this head of gold," had made a deep impression upon the ruler's mind. Verse 38. The wise men of his realm, taking advantage of this and of his return to idolatry, proposed that he make an image similar to the one seen in his dream, and set it up where all might behold the head of gold, which had been interpreted as representing his kingdom. *PK 504*

The worship of this image had been brought about by the wise men of Babylon in order to make the Hebrew youth join in their idolatrous worship. They were beautiful singers, and the Chaldeans wanted them to forget their God and accept the worship of the Babylonian idols. *ML 68*

CHAPTER 3 — The Clear and Present Paraphrase

1. After a while, Nebuchadnezzar decides to build a statue similar to what he saw in his dream. However, in an effort to challenge the prophecy and show that Babylon will last forever, he makes the whole statue out of gold! The image, which stands about 88 ft tall (including the platform) and 9 ft wide, is placed in the plains of Dura within the Babylonian territory.

2. Then Nebuchadnezzar orders all his officials to participate in the dedication of this image. This dedication includes princes, governors, commissioners, judges, treasurers, advisers, sheriffs, along with anyone else in an official position of authority. He summons all of them to this dedication ceremony.

3. All the princes, governors, commissioners, judges, treasurers, advisers, sheriffs, and other government officials arrive. They all stand before this image that Nebuchadnezzar set up.

4. Then Nebuchadnezzar's official announcer yells with a loud voice, "People of all nations, there is a command for you:

5. *That* at what time ye hear the sound of the cornet, flute, harp, sackbut, psaltery, dulcimer, and all kinds of musick, ye fall down and worship the golden image that Nebuchadnezzar the king hath set up:
6. And whoso falleth not down and worshippeth shall the same hour be cast into the midst of a burning fiery furnace.
7. Therefore at that time, when all the people heard the sound of the cornet, flute, harp, sackbut, psaltery, and all kinds of musick, all the people, the nations, and the languages, fell down *and* worshipped the golden image that Nebuchadnezzar the king had set up.
8. Wherefore at that time certain Chaldeans came near, and accused the Jews.

5. **Cornet** - Horn. **Flute** - pipe. **Sackbut** - The *sabbeka'* was a triangular instrument with four strings and a bright tone. **Psaltery** - The *psalterion* was a stringed triangular shape instrument, with the sounding board above the strings. **Dulcimer** – A bagpipe. **Worship the golden image** - The narrative said nothing about mandatory worship, only the image's dedication. However, the people may have understood by the invitation what that dedication entailed.
6. **Whoso falleth not down** - It is not certain where Daniel was at this time. It may be that the king sent Daniel on a journey to spare him the embarrassment. **Fiery furnace** - There are only a few of these kinds of death penalties on record; one example comes from Nergal-sharusur's (Nebuchadnezzar's son-in-law) inscription, which claims to burn to death his adversaries.
8. **Certain Chaldeans** - These weren't Jews. Instead, they were the class of wise men who Daniel previously saved.

EG White Notes

The appointed day came, and a vast concourse from all "people, nations, and languages," assembled on the plain of Dura. In harmony with the king's command, when the sound of music was heard, the whole company "fell down and worshipped the golden image." On that eventful day the powers of darkness seemed to be gaining a signal triumph; the worship of the golden image bade fair to become connected permanently with the established forms of idolatry recognized as the state religion of the land. Satan hoped thereby to defeat God's purpose of making the presence of captive Israel in Babylon a means of blessing to all the nations of heathendom. *PK 506*

Not all had bowed the knee to the idolatrous symbol of human power. In the midst of the worshipping multitude there were three men who were firmly resolved not thus to dishonor the God of heaven. *PK 506*

The Clear and Present Paraphrase

5. When you hear the sound of the horns, followed by the flutes, the various harps, bagpipes, and all other musical sounds, you are commanded to fall on your knees, bow to the ground, and worship this golden statue that King Nebuchadnezzar has set up.

6. Now, anyone who does not kneel down and worship will be executed on the spot by burning to death in a heated furnace."

7. Then the horns, flutes, and harps begin playing, and immediately the people fall down and begin worshipping Nebuchadnezzar's golden image.

8. While this is taking place, some of the Chaldeans watch the Hebrews hoping they'll be able to accuse them of being disloyal citizens.

9. They spake and said to the king Nebuchadnezzar, O king, live for ever.
10. Thou, O king, hast made a decree, that every man that shall hear the sound of the cornet, flute, harp, sackbut, psaltery, and dulcimer, and all kinds of musick, shall fall down and worship the golden image:
11. And whoso falleth not down and worshippeth, *that* he should be cast into the midst of a burning fiery furnace.
12. There are certain Jews whom thou hast set over the affairs of the province of Babylon, Shadrach, Meshach, and Abed-nego; these men, O king, have not regarded thee: they serve not thy gods, nor worship the golden image which thou hast set up.
13. Then Nebuchadnezzar in *his* rage and fury commanded to bring Shadrach, Meshach, and Abed-nego. Then they brought these men before the king.

9. **O king, live forever** - See in chapter 2:4
12. **Thou has set** - It seems the position these Chaldeans took against the Jews while referencing their exalted position suggests their denunciation arose from jealousy. Their words also contained hidden insinuations against the king, essentially blaming him for the lack of political foresight.
13. **Rage** - Violent anger

To Nebuchadnezzar, flushed with triumph, was brought the word that among his subjects there were some who dared disobey his mandate. Certain of the wise men, jealous of the honors that had been bestowed upon the faithful companions of Daniel, now reported to the king their flagrant violation of his wishes. *PK 506-507*

9. These same Chaldeans find their way to the king and say, "May Your Majesty live forever!
10. You commanded us that at the first sound of the horns, flutes, harps with other stringed instruments, bagpipes, and all the other musical sounds, everyone present should fall on their knees and bow in worship before your golden statue,
11. And that decree also states that anyone who didn't obey that command would immediately be executed by being thrown into the heated furnace.
12. Well, the three Jews you put in charge over the province of Babylon, Shadrach, Meshach, and Abednego, have disrespected you. Not only do they disregard our gods, but they even have the nerve to refuse to worship this image you have set up!!"
13. Nebuchadnezzar goes into a rage. He then orders his guards to bring Shadrach, Meshach, and Abednego to him at once.

Daniel 3

14. Nebuchadnezzar spake and said unto them, *Is it* true, O Shadrach, Meshach, and Abed-nego, do not ye serve my gods, nor worship the golden image which I have set up?
15. Now if ye be ready that at what time ye hear the sound of the cornet, flute, harp, sackbut, psaltery, and dulcimer, and all kinds of musick, ye fall down and worship the image which I have made; *well*: but if ye worship not, ye shall be cast the same hour into the midst of a burning fiery furnace; and who *is* that God that shall deliver you out of my hands?
16. Shadrach, Meshach, and Abed-nego, answered and said to the king, O Nebuchadnezzar, we *are* not careful to answer thee in this matter.

14. **Do not ye serve** - Here, the king referred to the first part of the Chaldean's accusation. Prior to this, the King had recognized Jehovah as a God of gods, but since a direct command had been disobeyed, the King's prior tolerance of the Jews worshipping Jehovah instead of the Pagan gods is probably seen as the cause for the "defiance" of Shadrach, Meshach, and Abednego.
15. **Who is that God** – King Nebuchadnezzar decides to directly challenge the power and authority of Jehovah while, at the same time, making the case that Jehovah was no stronger than the Pagan gods.
16. **Careful** - The response of the three Hebrew boys may be better translated: "We have no need to answer you in this matter." This may be seen as an act of defiance, but the three Hebrews did not deny the truth of the king's accusation; they just saw no reason to defend themselves or apologize.

EG White Notes

The king commanded that the men be brought before him. "Is it true," he inquired, "do not ye serve my gods, nor worship the golden image which I have set up?" He endeavored by threats to induce them to unite with the multitude. Pointing to the fiery furnace, he reminded them of the punishment awaiting them if they should persist in their refusal to obey his will. But firmly the Hebrews testified to their allegiance to the God of heaven, and their faith in His power to deliver. The act of bowing to the image was understood by all to be an act of worship. Such homage they could render to God alone. *PK 507*

As the three Hebrews stood before the king, he was convinced that they possessed something the other wise men of his kingdom did not have. They had been faithful in the performance of every duty. He would give them another trial. If only they would signify their willingness to unite with the multitude in worshiping the image, all would be well with them; "but if ye worship not," he added, "ye shall be cast the same hour into the midst of a burning fiery furnace." Then with his hand stretched upward in defiance, he demanded, "Who is that God that shall deliver you out of my hands?" *PK 507*

The Clear and Present Paraphrase

14. The guards bring the three Hebrews to the king, and he says to them, "Is it true, Shadrach, Meshach, and Abednego, that you are refusing to bow down and worship the golden statue that I have erected?"

15. He continues, "Listen very closely. I'm going to give you one more chance to demonstrate your loyalty to Babylon. Once the music begins playing and I see you bow down and worship the image, then all is forgiven; however, if you don't bow down and worship, I will burn all three of you alive inside of the furnace. Now, I don't know a god that can deliver you out of my hands...do you know of one?"

16. Shadrach, Meshach, and Abednego answer the king, "Your Majesty, it is not even necessary for us to defend ourselves in this matter because we have already made a decision.

17. If it be *so*, our God whom we serve is able to deliver us from the burning fiery furnace, and he will deliver *us* out of thine hand, O king.
18. But if not, be it known unto thee, O king, that we will not serve thy gods, nor worship the golden image which thou hast set up.
19. Then was Nebuchadnezzar full of fury, and the form of his visage was changed against Shadrach, Meshach, and Abed-nego: *therefore* he spake, and commanded that they should heat the furnace one seven times more than it was wont to be heated.
20. And he commanded the most mighty men that *were* in his army to bind Shadrach, Meshach, and Abed-nego, *and* to cast *them* into the burning fiery furnace.

17. **If it be so** - The "if" should not be taken as an indication of doubt in God's power to save, but as an indication of uncertainty as to whether it was God's will to save.
19. **One seven times more** - A strange construct, but this same form was also used in an Aramaic letter from the 5th century BC. The literal meaning is "seven times." The purpose of the unusual commandment was not to amplify the punishment, but rather to prevent any possible intervention of a supernatural order.
20. **The most mighty men** - The choice of military men of outstanding strength was most likely a result of Nebuchadnezzar anticipating that a supernatural intervention was possible.

EG White Notes

When the king saw that his will was not received as the will of God, he was "full of fury," and the form of his visage was changed against these men. Satanic attributes made his countenance appear as the countenance of a demon; and with all the force he could command, he ordered that the furnace be heated seven times hotter than its wont, and commanded the most mighty men to bind the youth, and cast them into the furnace. He felt that it required more than ordinary power to deal with these noble men. His mind was strongly impressed that something unusual would interpose in their behalf, and his strongest men were ordered to deal with them. *ST May 6, 1897*

The Clear and Present Paraphrase

17. You asked, do we know a god that can deliver us out of the fiery furnace. Well, the answer is yes. Our God, the One whom we worship, can deliver us from the burning furnace.
18. However, even if He chooses not to save us, one thing is guaranteed; we will not bow down and worship this golden image."
19. At this point, Nebuchadnezzar goes into a furious rage! His face becomes red with anger as he looks at Shadrach, Meshach, and Abednego. He then orders his men to make the furnace temperature seven times hotter than usual.
20. Once the furnace is hot enough, Nebuchadnezzar, in order to ensure nothing supernatural can intervene, commands some of his strongest men to tie up Shadrach, Meshach, and Abednego.

21. Then these men were bound in their coats, their hosen, and their hats, and their *other* garments, and were cast into the midst of the burning fiery furnace.
22. Therefore because the king's commandment was urgent, and the furnace exceeding hot, the flame of the fire slew those men that took up Shadrach, Meshach, and Abed-nego.
23. And these three men, Shadrach, Meshach, and Abed-nego, fell down bound into the midst of the burning fiery furnace.
24. Then Nebuchadnezzar the king was astonied, and rose up in haste, *and* spake, and said unto his counsellors, Did not we cast three men bound into the midst of the fire? They answered and said unto the king, True, O king.
25. He answered and said, Lo, I see four men loose, walking in the midst of the fire, and they have no hurt; and the form of the fourth is like the Son of God.

21. **Garments** - The articles of clothing, consisting of flammable material, were likely emphasizing the miracle that followed.
24. **Rose up in haste** - The king apparently had moved to the location of the execution to make sure that his command would be properly carried out. He was probably positioned to easily observe the victims as they were thrown into the fire.
25. **Like the Son of God** - Scholars differ on the meaning of this fourth individual in the fire. Jewish scholars have identified him as an angel, which view is also reflected in the LXX. However, most modern commentators translate the phrase, "like a son of the gods." In Aramaic, "gods" (*'Elahin*), is often referred to as pagan gods; however, there are two passages [Daniel 5:11,14] where it refers to the true God; therefore, "son of the gods," or "son of God," are both justifiable. However, since the context of Nebuchadnezzar's exclamation was in reference to the Most High God, the preferable interpretation is, "Like the Son of God."

EG White Notes

As His witnesses were cast into the furnace, the Saviour revealed Himself to them in person, and together they walked in the midst of the fire. In the presence of the Lord of heat and cold, the flames lost their power to consume. *PK 508-509*

The nobles standing near saw his face grow pale... In alarm the king, turning to his lords, asked, "Did not we cast three men bound into the midst of the fire? *PK 509*

... Lo, I see four men loose, walking in the midst of the fire, and they have no hurt; and the form of the fourth is like the Son of God." How did that heathen king know what the Son of God was like? The Hebrew captives filling positions of trust in Babylon had in life and character represented before him the truth. When asked for a reason of their faith, they had given it without hesitation. Plainly and simply they had presented the principles of righteousness, thus teaching those around them of the God whom they worshiped. They had told of Christ, the Redeemer to come; and in the form of the fourth in the midst of the fire the king recognized the Son of God. *PK 509*

The Clear and Present Paraphrase

21. These strongmen tie up the three Hebrews with full head-to-toe attire, including their robes, head coverings, and all other clothing; then, the strong men throw the three Hebrews into the blazing furnace.

22. The furnace is so hot that the strong men's clothes catch fire and burn them alive in the process of throwing the Hebrews into the furnace.

23. Shadrach, Meshach, and Abednego fall into the burning furnace while they are still tied up.

24. All of a sudden, Nebuchadnezzar jumps to his feet in total shock. He then turns to his advisers and says, "Correct me if I'm wrong, but didn't we throw three men into the furnace?" The advisers reply, "Yes, your Majesty, there were three men."

25. Nebuchadnezzar points to the burning furnace and cries out, "Look! Now there are four men...and they are all walking around inside the burning furnace unharmed!" Then Nebuchadnezzar looks a little closer at the furnace, and he says, "And the fourth one looks like the One they told me would come....the Son of God!"

26. Then Nebuchadnezzar came near to the mouth of the burning fiery furnace, *and* spake, and said, Shadrach, Meshach, and Abed-nego, ye servants of the most high God, come forth, and come *hither*. Then Shadrach, Meshach, and Abed-nego, came forth of the midst of the fire.

27. And the princes, governors, and captains, and the king's counsellors, being gathered together, saw these men, upon whose bodies the fire had no power, nor was an hair of their head singed, neither were their coats changed, nor the smell of fire had passed on them.

28. *Then* Nebuchadnezzar spake, and said, Blessed *be* the God of Shadrach, Meshach, and Abed-nego, who hath sent his angel, and delivered his servants that trusted in him, and have changed the king's word, and yielded their bodies, that they might not serve nor worship any god, except their own God.

26. **Most high God** - King Nebuchadnezzar's response did not imply that he had resigned from his Pagan believes, but rather he was acknowledging the God of Shadrach, Meshach, and Abednego as a chief God among all the other gods.

27. **The princes** - Concerning the officials mentioned in vs. 2.

28. **Blessed be the God** - The miraculous deliverance of the three Hebrews made a deep impression on the king and changed his previous opinion about the God of the Hebrews.

EG White Notes

And now, his own greatness and dignity forgotten, Nebuchadnezzar descended from his throne and, going to the mouth of the furnace, cried out, "Ye servants of the most high God, come forth, and come hither." Then Shadrach, Meshach, and Abednego came forth before the vast multitude, showing themselves unhurt. The presence of their Saviour had guarded them from harm, and only their fetters had been burned. *PK 509*

Forgotten was the great golden image, set up with such pomp. In the presence of the living God, men feared and trembled. "Blessed be the God of Shadrach, Meshach, and Abednego," the humbled king was constrained to acknowledge, "who hath sent His angel, and delivered His servants that trusted in Him, and have changed the king's word, and yielded their bodies, that they might not serve nor worship any god, except their own God." *PK 510*

The Clear and Present Paraphrase

26. Then the king walks as close to the door of the furnace as possible, and he calls out to the three Hebrews, "Shadrach, Meshach, Abednego, servants of the Most High God, get out of the furnace and come here." Then they all stand there and watch as Shadrach, Meshach, and Abednego walk right out of the furnace.

27. As the Hebrews walk out of the furnace, everyone crowds around to examine them. Not only is their skin free of burns and blisters, but their hair shows no evidence of being in the fire, and they don't even smell like smoke!

28. Then Nebuchadnezzar shouts, "Praise to the God of Shadrach, Meshach, and Abednego who sent His Angel to deliver them out of my hands. They trusted in Him, and their loyalty is why they disobeyed my orders and risked their lives, rather than bowing and worshipping a deity that's not their God.

KJV Bible

29. Therefore I make a decree, That every people, nation, and language, which speak any thing amiss against the God of Shadrach, Meshach, and Abed-nego, shall be cut in pieces, and their houses shall be made a dunghill: because there is no other God that can deliver after this sort.

30. Then the king promoted Shadrach, Meshach, and Abed-nego, in the province of Babylon.

Daniel Commentary

29. I make a decree - While some may view this as a favorable decree, Nebuchadnezzar exceeded his rights when he sought by force to compel men to honor the God of the Hebrews. **Cut in pieces** - On the penalties here threatened (see chapter 2:5).

30. Promoted – Meaning, "To cause to prosper," and in the broader sense, "to promote." How this promotion was carried out is not mentioned in scripture; however, the three Hebrews may have received money, or more influence and power in the province's administration, or more elevated titles.

EG White Notes

In these and like words the king of Babylon endeavored to spread abroad before all the peoples of earth his conviction that the power and authority of the God of the Hebrews was worthy of supreme adoration. And God was pleased with the effort of the king to show Him reverence, and to make the royal confession of allegiance as widespread as was the Babylonian realm.

It was right for the king to make public confession, and to seek to exalt the God of heaven above all other gods; but in endeavoring to force his subjects to make a similar confession of faith and to show similar reverence, Nebuchadnezzar was exceeding his right as a temporal sovereign. He had no more right, either civil or moral, to threaten men with death for not worshiping God, than he had to make the decree consigning to the flames all who refused to worship the golden image. God never compels the obedience of man. He leaves all free to choose whom they will serve. *PK 510-512*

The Clear and Present Paraphrase

29. Therefore, I'm going to make the following law: Regardless of where you are born or what language you speak, if anyone says anything remotely disrespectful about the God of Shadrach, Meshach, and Abednego, he will be ripped in pieces, limb from limb and his house will be made a public place for human waste. The reason for this law is because no other god can deliver people the way their God delivered them."

30. Then the king promotes Shadrach, Meshach, and Abednego, making them even greater throughout Babylon.

DANIEL 3 - TEST YOUR KNOWLEDGE

1. What did the statue made of all gold represent to Nebuchadnezzar? (*p. 54*) ___
   _____

2. True or False: The Jews were exempt from having to bow to the image? (*p. 55*)

3. What was the motive behind Nebuchadnezzar's wise men informing him that the Hebrew had defied his orders? (*p. 59*)_____
   _____

4. Why did the king make the fire seven times hotter? (*pp. 62-63*)_____
   _____

5. True or False - Gabriel showed up in the fire with the three Hebrew boys. (*pp. 64-65*)

6. How did Nebuchadnezzar know about the Son of God? (*p. 65*)_____
   _____

7. What happened to the men that threw the Hebrew boys into the fire? (*p. 64*)
   _____

8. After Nebuchadnezzar's dream was revealed to him, he was initially influenced by the fear of God. Why did he change? (*p. 55*)_____
   _____

9. What attributes made Nebuchadnezzar's countenance appear like a demon? (*p. 63*)_____

10. Ellen White says, "God never compels the _____ of a man. (*p. 69*)

Questions for Discussion:

1. Why wasn't Daniel in the fiery furnace with his friends? Do you believe Daniel bowed to the idol?

2. Couldn't the Hebrew boys just pretended to pick something off the ground to give the appearance of worship? Would that still constitute worship?

3. Why did Nebuchadnezzar keep going back into sin after all the miracles he had seen? Do we have the same problem?

King Nebuchadnezzar forgets that God is the One who places kings on their thrones, therefore God decides to give the king a seven-year reminder.

Daniel 4

The Humbling of King Nebuchadnezzar

CHAPTER 4

1. Nebuchadnezzar the king, unto all people, nations, and languages, that dwell in all the earth; Peace be multiplied unto you.
2. I thought it good to shew the signs and wonders that the high God hath wrought toward me.
3. How great *are* his signs! and how mighty *are* his wonders! his kingdom *is* an everlasting kingdom, and his dominion *is* from generation to generation.
4. I Nebuchadnezzar was at rest in mine house, and flourishing in my palace:
5. I saw a dream which made me afraid, and the thoughts upon my bed and the visions of my head troubled me.
6. Therefore made I a decree to bring in all the wise *men* of Babylon before me, that they might make known unto me the interpretation of the dream.

CHAPTER 4

1. **Unto all people** - This chapter is conveyed in the form of a royal proclamation. The change in this chapter from the first person to the third person and back again to the first person has been explained by assuming either Daniel wrote the edict by command of the king or that, as his chief counselor, Daniel added certain portions to the proclamation written by the king.
4. **At rest** - This phrase possibly means the king had undisturbed possession of the kingdom.
5. **Afraid** - This abrupt introduction of this event illustrates the unexpected suddenness of the situation.
6. **Decree** - During the dream of chapter 2, the wise men were summoned. However, in this instance, the king remembered his dream, so his demands were significantly different.

CHAPTER 4

EG White Notes

Nebuchadnezzar's noble conception of God's purpose concerning the nations was lost sight of later in his experience; yet when his proud spirit was humbled before the multitude on the plain of Dura, he once more had acknowledged that God's kingdom is "an everlasting kingdom, and His dominion is from generation to generation." An idolater by birth and training, and at the head of an idolatrous people, he had nevertheless an innate sense of justice and right, and God was able to use him as an instrument for the punishment of the rebellious and for the fulfillment of the divine purpose. "The terrible of the nations" (Ezekiel 28:7), it was given Nebuchadnezzar, after years of patient and wearing labor, to conquer Tyre; Egypt also fell a prey to his victorious armies; and as he added nation after nation to the Babylonian realm, he added more and more to his fame as the greatest ruler of the age.
PK 514

CHAPTER 4

The Clear and Present Paraphrase

1. Nebuchadnezzar sends this message to all nations and language groups in his kingdom and nations he had conquered: Peace to all of you.
2. I want to testify of all the great miracles and wonderful things that the God of heaven has done for me.
3. What a great and wonderful God He is! His miracles are nothing short of incredible! His kingdom is the only kingdom that will last throughout the ceaseless ages of eternity.
4. Here's my testimony: A little over seven years ago, I, Nebuchadnezzar, was relaxing in my palace thinking about all my accomplishments and was feeling quite good about myself.
5. I dozed off and had a dream which turned into a nightmare. I was very frightened by the dream, and on top of that, I couldn't get the terrible images out of my head.
6. So, once again, I called all the wise men of Babylon to stand in my presence in order to get the interpretation of my dream.

7. Then came in the magicians, the astrologers, the Chaldeans, and the soothsayers: and I told the dream before them; but they did not make known unto me the interpretation thereof.
8. But at the last Daniel came in before me, whose name *was* Belteshazzar, according to the name of my god, and in whom *is* the spirit of the holy gods: and before him I told the dream, *saying*,
9. O Belteshazzar, master of the magicians, because I know that the spirit of the holy gods *is* in thee, and no secret troubleth thee, tell me the visions of my dream that I have seen, and the interpretation thereof.

7. **Did not make known** - It has been suggested that because these wise men were considered experts in interpreting signs and dreams, they likely attempted to interpret the dream; however, even if they did offer an explanation, it was clearly rejected by the king.
8. **Belteshazzar** - He is introduced by his Jewish name, then by his Babylonian name. We aren't told why Daniel had been kept in the background even though he was the "master of the magicians." Some have suggested the king wanted to find out what the Chaldeans had to say first before hearing the truth. **Of the holy gods** – Also "of the holy God." A term frequently applied to false gods, but can also apply to the true God (see Dan 3:25).
9. **Master of the magicians** - The word "master" in chapter 4:9 and "chief" in chapter 2:48 are translations of the same Aramaic word, *rab*.

EG White Notes

Greatly troubled by the dream, which was evidently a prediction of adversity, the king repeated it to "the magicians, the astrologers, the Chaldeans, and the soothsayers;" but although the dream was very explicit, none of the wise men could interpret it.

Once more in this idolatrous nation, testimony was to be borne to the fact that only those who love and fear God can understand the mysteries of the kingdom of heaven. The king in his perplexity sent for his servant Daniel, a man esteemed for his integrity and constancy and for his unrivaled wisdom. *PK 516*

When Daniel, in response to the royal summons, stood in the king's presence, Nebuchadnezzar said, "O Belteshazzar, master of the magicians, because I know that the spirit of the holy gods is in thee, and no secret troubleth thee, tell me the visions of my dream that I have seen, and the interpretation thereof." *PK 517*

The Clear and Present Paraphrase

7. And, once again, they could not interpret my dream, even after I was able to tell them what happened in the dream!

8. Finally, I called Daniel, whom I named Belteshazzar after my god because I know the gods' spirit is with him. He arrived in my presence, and I told him my dream. Here is what I told him:

9. "Chief of the governors over all the wise men of Babylon, I know that the spirit of the holy gods is with you, and they keep nothing hidden from you. I have had another dream. I want you to listen to what I have seen and tell me its meaning.

10. Thus *were* the visions of mine head in my bed; I saw, and behold a tree in the midst of the earth, and the height thereof *was* great.
11. The tree grew, and was strong, and the height thereof reached unto heaven, and the sight thereof to the end of all the earth:
12. The leaves thereof *were* fair, and the fruit thereof much, and in it *was* meat for all: the beasts of the field had shadow under it, and the fowls of the heaven dwelt in the boughs thereof, and all flesh was fed of it.
13. I saw in the visions of my head upon my bed, and, behold, a watcher and an holy one came down from heaven;
14. He cried aloud, and said thus, Hew down the tree, and cut off his branches, shake off his leaves, and scatter his fruit: let the beasts get away from under it, and the fowls from his branches:

10. **Behold a tree** - God often uses parables as a method for revealing the truth. Parables often help recipients retain messages in their memory longer than if the message was communicated using other methods.
11. **Heaven** - The word in the original language can be translated as the visible sky or the unseen place where God dwells.
12. **Flesh** - All living creatures.
13. **A watcher and an holy one** -The LXX translates this as "angel" while other translations contain variations of "watcher." This much is evident: The watcher was recognized as having the credentials of the God of heaven.
14. **Hew down**– To cut down

EG White Notes

The dream given at this time to the king of Babylon was a very striking one. In a vision of the night he saw a great tree growing in the midst of the earth, towering to the heavens, and its branches stretching to the ends of the earth. "The leaves thereof were fair, and the fruit thereof much, and in it was meat for all: the beasts of the field had shadow under it, and the fowls of the heaven dwelt in the boughs thereof, and all flesh was fed of it."

As the king gazed upon that lofty tree, he beheld "a Watcher," even "an Holy One,"—a divine Messenger, similar in appearance to the One who walked with the Hebrews in the fiery furnace. This heavenly Being approached the tree, and in a loud voice cried:

"Hew down the tree, and cut off his branches, shake off his leaves, and scatter his fruit; let the beasts get away from under it, and the fowls from his branches... *YI November 1, 1904*

The Clear and Present Paraphrase

10. I fell asleep in my palace, and while I was sleeping, I dreamed that I saw a huge tree standing in the middle of the earth. This tree was the biggest tree that I had ever seen in my life.

11. As I watched, the tree grew bigger, and it seemed that the top of the tree reached all the way to outer space. As a matter of fact, it was so tall that everyone on the earth could see this tree.

12. The leaves were beautiful, and there was a lot of fruit...so much fruit that it could feed everyone! This tree provided shade for the animals of the field and a home for all the birds of the air. Everyone received their nourishment from this tree.

13. I dreamed all of this while lying in bed, but then a holy angel from heaven came down and visited me.

14. Then, with a loud voice, this angel said, 'Chop this tree down, trim its leaves, and scatter its fruit. Drive away the animals receiving its shade and shoo away the birds living in its branches.

15. Nevertheless leave the stump of his roots in the earth, even with a band of iron and brass, in the tender grass of the field; and let it be wet with the dew of heaven, and *let* his portion *be* with the beasts in the grass of the earth:

16. Let his heart be changed from man's, and let a beast's heart be given unto him; and let seven times pass over him.

17. This matter *is* by the decree of the watchers, and the demand by the word of the holy ones: to the intent that the living may know that the most High ruleth in the kingdom of men, and giveth it to whomsoever he will, and setteth up over it the basest of men.

18. This dream I king Nebuchadnezzar have seen. Now thou, O Belteshazzar, declare the interpretation thereof, forasmuch as all the wise *men* of my kingdom are not able to make known unto me the interpretation: but thou *art* able; for the spirit of the holy gods *is* in thee.

15. **Leave the stump** - This root-stump typified King Nebuchadnezzar's restoration from his sickness, not the continued supremacy of his dynasty, as some commentators have explained it. The whole passage obviously refers to an individual and not a nation.

16. **His heart** - The term "heart" here seems to indicate nature. The King would take on the nature of a beast. **Seven times** - A majority of scholars interpret "time" as "years."

17. **Watchers** - Heavenly council or assembly (see Job 1:6-12) **The most High ruleth** - In the affairs of nations, God is always working out the counsels of His own will. **Basest** - "lowly", "humble."

18. **The holy gods** - See on vs. 8.

After relating the dream, Nebuchadnezzar said: "O Belteshazzar, declare the interpretation thereof, forasmuch as all the wise men of my kingdom are not able to make known unto me the interpretation: but thou art able; for the spirit of the holy gods is in thee."
PK 517

15. But make sure you leave the stump and the roots. Place iron and bronze bands around the stump to preserve it and leave the grass around it as he will share the same habitat as the animals in the wild.

16. His ability to reason like a human will be taken from him, and in return, he will become deranged and wild like an animal. He will remain in this condition for the next seven years.

17. This was all decided by the heavenly assembly of watchers so that the world will know that The Most High is the ultimate ruler of this earth, and it is He that allows men to become king, even the lowest of humanity if He so chooses.'

18. So, Daniel, this was the dream that I had. Now, please tell me what all this means because all the wise men in Babylon are clueless; but I know from our experiences together that you have power from the holy gods, and they will tell you what all this means."

19. Then Daniel, whose name *was* Belteshazzar, was astonied for one hour, and his thoughts troubled him. The king spake, and said, Belteshazzar, let not the dream, or the interpretation thereof, trouble thee. Belteshazzar answered and said, My lord, the dream *be* to them that hate thee, and the interpretation thereof to thine enemies.

20. The tree that thou sawest, which grew, and was strong, whose height reached unto the heaven, and the sight thereof to all the earth;

21. Whose leaves *were* fair, and the fruit thereof much, and in it *was* meat for all; under which the beasts of the field dwelt, and upon whose branches the fowls of the heaven had their habitation:

22. It *is* thou, O king, that art grown and become strong: for thy greatness is grown, and reacheth unto heaven, and thy dominion to the end of the earth.

19. **Astonied** - "to be perplexed" or "to be embarrassed." **Hour** - This may be a brief moment or a longer period of time. Either way, sufficient time must have elapsed for Daniel to have revealed that "his thoughts troubled him." It appears Daniel was searching for suitable words to break the terrible news concerning the king's future fate. **The king spake** - Critics note the king now speaks in the third person, which has caused some to question the authenticity of this story; however, similar changes from the first to third person and vice versa are found in other books (see Ezra 7:13-15; Esther 8:7-8).

22. **It is thou** - Daniel goes straight to the point and announces that the tree represents the king himself. **Unto heaven** - To some, Daniel seems to be exaggerating Nebuchadnezzar's greatness; however, we must bear in mind that Daniel used east Asian court language and idioms, to which both he and the king were accustomed.

EG White Notes

The prophet realized that God had laid on him the solemn duty of revealing to Nebuchadnezzar the judgment about to fall upon him because of his pride and arrogance. Although its dreadful import had made him hesitate, he must state the truth, whatever the consequences to himself. *FSTS 269*

To Daniel the meaning of the dream was plain, and its significance startled him. Seeing Daniel's hesitation and distress, the king expressed sympathy for his servant. "Let not the dream, or the interpretation thereof, trouble thee." *PK 517*

Then Daniel made known the mandate of the Almighty. "The tree that thou sawest," he said, "which grew, and was strong, whose height reached unto the heaven, and the sight thereof to all the earth; whose leaves were fair, and the fruit thereof much, and in it was meat for all; under which the beast of the field dwelt, and upon whose branches the fowls of the heaven had their habitation: it is thou, O king, that art grown and become strong: for thy greatness is grown, and reacheth unto heaven, and thy dominion to the end of the earth. *PK 517*

The Clear and Present Paraphrase

19. Then there's an awkward silence. Daniel knows the meaning of the dream but is stunned when he realizes the magnitude of its fulfillment. King Nebuchadnezzar, sensing Daniel's hesitation, breaks the silence and says, "Belteshazzar, I can tell by your hesitation that the dream is bad news for me." Daniel remains quiet. Nebuchadnezzar continues, "but I can take it; don't let it bother you... just tell me what it means." Then Daniel, while looking into the eyes of the king, says, "My Lord, I sure wish this dream applied to your enemies and those that are against you!

20. However, the tree that you saw grow strong and tall...so tall that anyone who looked at the sky could see it;

21. Which had beautiful leaves and was bearing many fruits for everyone, under which the animals of the field came to rest and where the birds built their nests;

22. Well, my Lord," Daniel continues, "that tree represents you. You see, just like that tree, you have become great and strong. And just like that tree, you can be seen by everyone, and your dominion spreads throughout the world.

23. And whereas the king saw a watcher and an holy one coming down from heaven, and saying, Hew the tree down, and destroy it; yet leave the stump of the roots thereof in the earth, even with a band of iron and brass, in the tender grass of the field; and let it be wet with the dew of heaven, and *let* his portion *be* with the beasts of the field, till seven times pass over him;

24. This *is* the interpretation, O king, and this *is* the decree of the most High, which is come upon my lord the king:

25. That they shall drive thee from men, and thy dwelling shall be with the beasts of the field, and they shall make thee to eat grass as oxen, and they shall wet thee with the dew of heaven, and seven times shall pass over thee, till thou know that the most High ruleth in the kingdom of men, and giveth it to whomsoever he will.

25. **With the beasts -** The reason for his removal from society is not stated, though most likely understood by the king. It's apparent that the judgment was insanity; this can be concluded not only from the general remarks of this verse describing his future status but also from verses later on in this chapter that says his "understanding returned" (vs. 34).

EG White Notes

"And whereas the king saw a Watcher and an Holy One coming down from heaven, and saying, Hew the tree down, and destroy it; yet leave the stump of the roots thereof in the earth, even with a band of iron and brass, in the tender grass of the field; and let it be wet with the dew of heaven, and let his portion be with the beasts of the field, till seven times pass over him; this is the interpretation, O king, and this is the decree of the Most High, which is come upon my lord the king: that they shall drive thee from men, and thy dwelling shall be with the beasts of the field, and they shall make thee to eat grass as oxen, and they shall wet thee with the dew of heaven, and seven times shall pass over thee, till thou know that the Most High ruleth in the kingdom of men, and giveth it to whomsoever He will." *PK 518*

The Clear and Present Paraphrase

23. My Lord, then you saw an angel, which said, 'Cut down the tree and destroy it but leave the stump and the roots. Put a band of iron and bronze around it and let it get wet with the morning dew like the grass of the field. Whoever represents this tree will live with the animals for seven years.'"

24. Daniel looks directly at the king and says, "So that's what your dream meant. The Most High God has decreed this to happen to you, my Lord.

25. Your mind will leave you, resulting in your being driven away from society. You will begin to think like an animal, and you will dwell with animals in the fields. You'll do everything like them; you'll eat like them, you'll sleep like them, you'll live like them. All of this will take place for the next seven years until you learn that God is the true Ruler of this world's Empires, and whoever He chooses, that individual will rule the known world.

26. And whereas they commanded to leave the stump of the tree roots; thy kingdom shall be sure unto thee, after that thou shalt have known that the heavens do rule.
27. Wherefore, O king, let my counsel be acceptable unto thee, and break off thy sins by righteousness, and thine iniquities by shewing mercy to the poor; if it may be a lengthening of thy tranquillity.
28. All this came upon the king Nebuchadnezzar.
29. At the end of twelve months he walked in the palace of the kingdom of Babylon.
30. The king spake, and said, Is not this great Babylon, that I have built for the house of the kingdom by the might of my power, and for the honour of my majesty?

26. **Shall be sure** - Many have wondered why Nebuchadnezzar was not killed or replaced while his mind was gone. The likely reason is that superstitious ancients thought that evil spirits caused all mental disturbances, and whoever killed that individual would become possessed with the same spirit. *SDA Bible Commentary Vol 4, p. 792*
27. **Break off thy sins** - God announced the judgment upon Nebuchadnezzar but gave him a full year to repent and prevent the foreseen tragedy. **Shewing mercy** - The king was warned that he needed to practice righteousness toward all his subjects and exercise mercy toward the oppressed, miserable, and poor.
29. **In the Palace** - Literally, "upon the palace."
30. **That I have built** - This must not be interpreted as a reference to the establishment of Babylon. Nimrod is the one who founded the city (also called Babel) shortly after the flood. Nebuchadnezzar's reference is to the great work of rebuilding Babylon, which his father, Nabopolassar, began, and Nebuchadnezzar completed.

EG White Notes

Daniel urged the proud monarch to repent... *FSTS 269*

For a time the impression of the warning and the counsel of the prophet was strong upon Nebuchadnezzar; but the heart that is not transformed by the grace of God soon loses the impressions of the Holy Spirit. Self-indulgence and ambition had not yet been eradicated from the king's heart, and later on these traits reappeared. Notwithstanding the instruction so graciously given him, and the warnings of past experience, Nebuchadnezzar again allowed himself to be controlled by a spirit of jealousy against the kingdoms that were to follow. His rule, which heretofore had been to a great degree just and merciful, became oppressive. Hardening his heart, he used his God-given talents for self-glorification, exalting himself above the God who had given him life and power...A year from the time he had received the warning, Nebuchadnezzar, walking in his palace and thinking with pride of his power as a ruler and of his success as a builder, exclaimed, "Is not this great Babylon, that I have built for the house of the kingdom by the might of my power, and for the honor of my majesty?" *PK 519*

The Clear and Present Paraphrase

26. However, your kingdom will be restored back to you, which is why the stump and the roots remained. However, this will only happen after you acknowledge God's supremacy.

27. Now, if I may advise you, my Lord, please show your repentance by doing right; show mercy to the oppressed, and perhaps the Lord will shorten your punishment."

28. Unfortunately, the king doesn't listen to Daniel, and events happen to him, just as Daniel prophesied.

29. About one year later, King Nebuchadnezzar is taking a walk on the roof of his palace.

30. As he's walking and observing the breathtaking views, he suddenly stops; his eyes pan over the whole city, and he fills up with pride exclaiming to himself, "This is the great Babylon! And I am the one who built it!! This is the most glorious kingdom that has ever existed, and it was because of my intelligence! It was because of my might and power and superiority!"

KJV Bible	Daniel Commentary
31. While the word *was* in the king's mouth, there fell a voice from heaven, *saying*, O king Nebuchadnezzar, to thee it is spoken; The kingdom is departed from thee.	31. **There fell a voice** - It is not stated whether this voice was heard by Nebuchadnezzar alone or whether everyone with him also heard the voice.
32. And they shall drive thee from men, and thy dwelling *shall be* with the beasts of the field: they shall make thee to eat grass as oxen, and seven times shall pass over thee, until thou know that the most High ruleth in the kingdom of men, and giveth it to whomsoever he will.	32. **Seven times** - See vs. 16. It's also interesting to note that the same king who called for the fire to be seven times hotter will now eat with the beasts of the fields for a period of "seven times."
33. The same hour was the thing fulfilled upon Nebuchadnezzar: and he was driven from men, and did eat grass as oxen, and his body was wet with the dew of heaven, till his hairs were grown like eagles' *feathers*, and his nails like birds' *claws*.	33. **Fulfilled** - It is unnecessary to identify King Nebuchadnezzar's condition precisely or equate it with anything known to medical science today. The experience may have been unique. **Eagles' feathers** - When uncombed and with extended exposure to the influences of rough weather and sunlight, hair can become stiff and unruly.
34. And at the end of the days I Nebuchadnezzar lifted up mine eyes unto heaven, and mine understanding returned unto me, and I blessed the most High, and I praised and honoured him that liveth for ever, whose dominion *is* an everlasting dominion, and his kingdom *is* from generation to generation:	34. **End of the days** - The end of the seven years. **Lifted up mine eyes** - It is important to notice that the return of the king's mind coincides with his recognition of the true God. When the humbled king prayerfully looked to heaven, he was elevated from that of a brute beast to that of a being bearing the image of God.

EG White Notes

Here we are shown that God holds even heathen kings subject to his will. He takes idolaters, and deals with them according to their evil ways and doings. *YI May 19, 1898*

In a moment the reason that God had given him was taken away; the judgment that the king thought perfect, the wisdom on which he prided himself, was removed, and the once mighty ruler was a maniac. His hand could no longer sway the scepter. The messages of warning had been unheeded; now, stripped of the power his Creator had given him, and driven from men, Nebuchadnezzar "did eat grass as oxen, and his body was wet with the dew of heaven, till his hairs were grown like eagles' feathers, and his nails like birds' claws." For seven years Nebuchadnezzar was an astonishment to all his subjects; for seven years he was humbled before all the world. *PK 520*

Then his reason was restored and, looking up in humility to the God of heaven, he recognized the divine hand in his chastisement. *PK 520*

The Clear and Present Paraphrase

31. As soon as he makes this statement, he hears a voice saying, "King Nebuchadnezzar, your kingdom has just been taken from you.

32. You will lose your mind and be driven from society to live with the animals of the field. For the next seven years, you will eat grass like an ox until you learn that the Most High God rules in the affairs of men and can give your kingdom to whomever he wants."

33. Immediately, Nebuchadnezzar begins losing his mind. Once his advisors realize what's happening, they take him to the fields, where he begins eating grass just like an ox. His body becomes wet with the morning dew, his hair becomes matted and unruly, and his fingernails grow like bird's claws.

34. Then, after seven years, the king's mind suddenly comes back to him. Once he realizes his sanity is back, he stands in the open field, looks up to heaven, and begins praising God, saying, "I praise and worship the One who lives forever! Only His reign lasts forever; only His kingdom endures from generation to generation!

35. And all the inhabitants of the earth *are* reputed as nothing: and he doeth according to his will in the army of heaven, and *among* the inhabitants of the earth: and none can stay his hand, or say unto him, What doest thou?

36. At the same time my reason returned unto me; and for the glory of my kingdom, mine honour and brightness returned unto me; and my counsellors and my lords sought unto me; and I was established in my kingdom, and excellent majesty was added unto me.

37. Now I Nebuchadnezzar praise and extol and honour the King of heaven, all whose works *are* truth, and his ways judgment: and those that walk in pride he is able to abase.

35. **As nothing** - Compare Isaiah 40:17. Some have suggested that, in his association with Daniel, the king had become acquainted with Isaiah's words and that he suddenly recalled those words.

36. **Returned unto me** - With the restoration of his mind, King Nebuchadnezzar also regained his royal dignity and his throne. **Sought unto me** - Sought doesn't necessarily mean that the king wandered around the fields unsupervised during his period of insanity, but rather this denotes they went looking for the king with the sole purpose of restoring him to his official position. When it became known that the king's mind had returned, the regents of Babylon brought him back with all due respect so that they might restore the government to him again. These regents are likely the same men that carried on the government's affairs during the king's seven-year hiatus.

37. **Praise and extol** - Nebuchadnezzar finally recognized the righteousness of God. His confession that God is "King of heaven" expressed his respect towards God.

EG White Notes

The once proud monarch had become a humble child of God; the tyrannical, overbearing ruler, a wise and compassionate king. He who had defied and blasphemed the God of heaven, now acknowledged the power of the Most High and earnestly sought to promote the fear of Jehovah and the happiness of his subjects. Under the rebuke of Him who is King of kings and Lord of lords, Nebuchadnezzar had learned at last the lesson which all rulers need to learn—that true greatness consists in true goodness. He acknowledged Jehovah as the living God, saying, "I Nebuchadnezzar praise and extol and honor the King of heaven, all whose works are truth, and His ways judgment: and those that walk in pride He is able to abase." *PK 521*

The Clear and Present Paraphrase

35. Everyone else is irrelevant! It doesn't matter if it's heaven or earth; His sovereignty is everywhere! Who is powerful enough to stop Him? Who is wise enough to question Him?"

36. Once King Nebuchadnezzar's closest advisers get word that their king's mind is back, they, with open arms, get him out of the fields in order to restore him to his rightful place on the throne. Everyone is so happy to have him back, and it becomes apparent that he is viewed even more honorably than before the ordeal.

37. Nebuchadnezzar comes to one conclusion after all this takes place. He proclaims, "I, Nebuchadnezzar, praise and honor the God of heaven, and I glorify the King of kings, whose ways are right and just toward everyone but who also humbles those who are lifted up by pride and power."

DANIEL 4 - TEST YOUR KNOWLEDGE

1. What was behind Nebuchadnezzar's spirit of jealously? (*p. 87*) _____

   _____

2. Who did the tree represent? (*pp. 82-83*) _____

3. Who did Nebuchadnezzar first call after his dream? (*pp. 74*) _____

4. Where was Nebuchadnezzar when he had this vision/ dream? (*pp.74-75*) ____

   _____

5. Explain what Nebuchadnezzar saw in his dream. (*p. 78*) _____

   _____

   _____

6. What was Daniel's reaction when he understood the meaning of the king's vision/ dream? (*pp. 82*) _____

7. How many years was Nebuchadnezzar to dwell with the beasts of the field? (*pp. 84-85*) _____

8. What did God want Nebuchadnezzar to realize before he would be reinstated as king? (*p. 84*) _____

9. Why did Daniel tell the king to break off his sins? (*p.86*) _____

   _____

10. What does Nebuchadnezzar say God is able to do to those who walk in pride? (*p. 90*) _____

Questions for Discussion:

1. Do you believe God interacted with other kings as he did with Nebuchadnezzar? Why?

2. We see that God humbled Nebuchadnezzar until he learned his lesson. Do you believe God humbles us in this same way today?

Belshazzar refuses to give God the glory. He will even get to the point of mocking God. In the end, Belshazzar will learn the same lesson his grandfather, King Nebuchadnezzar, learned— God sets kings up, and He can take them down.

Daniel 5

The Handwriting on the Wall

CHAPTER 5

1. Belshazzar the king made a great feast to a thousand of his lords, and drank wine before the thousand.
2. Belshazzar, whiles he tasted the wine, commanded to bring the golden and silver vessels which his father Nebuchadnezzar had taken out of the temple which *was* in Jerusalem; that the king, and his princes, his wives, and his concubines, might drink therein.
3. Then they brought the golden vessels that were taken out of the temple of the house of God which *was* at Jerusalem; and the king, and his princes, his wives, and his concubines, drank in them.
4. They drank wine, and praised the gods of gold, and of silver, of brass, of iron, of wood, and of stone.

CHAPTER 5

1. **The king** - Belshazzar was the eldest son of Nabonidus (Scholars dispute Belshazzar being called "The King" because history records the last king of Babylon as Nabonidus). However, history also documents that Nabonidus summoned his eldest son, Belshazzar, and entrusted the kingship to him before setting out on a war campaign. So, from this time on, Belshazzar controlled the affairs of Babylonia as co-ruler.
2. **His father** - Belshazzar's mother, was Nebuchadnezzar's daughter, which means Nebuchadnezzar was Belshazzar's grandfather. The word "father" must be understood to mean "grandfather" or "ancestor," as in many other passages in the Bible (see 1Chronicles 2:7).
3. **His wives, and his concubines** - It appears that the "queen" was not found among the disorderly drinkers.
4. **Praise the gods** - These were the songs that the drunken idol worshippers sang in honor of their Babylonian gods, whose images adorned numerous temples around the city.

CHAPTER 5

Through the folly and weakness of Belshazzar, the grandson of Nebuchadnezzar, proud Babylon was soon to fall. Admitted in his youth to a share in kingly authority, Belshazzar gloried in his power and lifted up his heart against the God of heaven. Many had been his opportunities to know the divine will and to understand his responsibility of rendering obedience thereto. He had known of his grandfather's banishment, by the decree of God, from the society of men; and he was familiar with Nebuchadnezzar's conversion and miraculous restoration. But Belshazzar allowed the love of pleasure and self-glorification to efface the lessons that he should never have forgotten. He wasted the opportunities graciously granted him, and neglected to use the means within his reach for becoming more fully acquainted with truth. *PK 522*

CHAPTER 5

1. It's now several years later. Nebuchadnezzar is dead, and his grandson, Belshazzar, is co-ruler with his father, King Nabonidus. On this particular day, King Belshazzar decides to throw a big party to which he invites one thousand of the most important people in Babylon. Princes, wealthy statesmen, and beautiful women are all there, drinking and dancing the night away.

2. It's at that moment an intoxicated Belshazzar gets an idea. He orders his guards to bring in the gold and silver cups that his grandfather, Nebuchadnezzar, took from the Temple in Jerusalem so that he and all his guests can drink from them.

3. The guards leave and come back shortly afterward and in their hands are the golden cups from the temple. They pour wine into the cups and start drinking. If that's not enough, while they are drinking, they begin to praise the gods of Babylon.

4. They continue to drink as they direct their praise towards the gods of gold, and of silver, of brass, of iron, of wood, and of stone.

5. In the same hour came forth fingers of a man's hand, and wrote over against the candlestick upon the plaister of the wall of the king's palace: and the king saw the part of the hand that wrote.

6. Then the king's countenance was changed, and his thoughts troubled him, so that the joints of his loins were loosed, and his knees smote one against another.

7. The king cried aloud to bring in the astrologers, the Chaldeans, and the soothsayers. *And* the king spake, and said to the wise *men* of Babylon, Whosoever shall read this writing, and shew me the interpretation thereof, shall be clothed with scarlet, and *have* a chain of gold about his neck, and shall be the third ruler in the kingdom.

5. **Upon the plaister** - The walls were covered with white plaster made of fine plaster of Paris (SDA Bible Commentary Vol 4 pg. 802). It's not explained whether the writing took the form of painted letters or was incised in the plaster. **Part of the hand** - We are not told how much of the hand was visible.

6. **Were loosed** - Compare Isaiah 21:3.

7. **Scarlet** - Royal purple was a deep purple reddish color. **Chain of gold** - The custom of honoring favorite public servants of the crown with gold chains existed in Egypt many centuries earlier (see Genesis 41:42). **Third ruler** - With his father, Nabonidus, occupying the throne as the first ruler, and Belshazzar occupying the slot for the second ruler, it is clear why Belshazzar could bestow no higher position in the realm than that of the "third ruler."

EG White Notes

When the revelry was at its height a bloodless hand came forth and traced upon the walls of the palace characters that gleamed like fire—words which, though unknown to the vast throng, were a portent of doom to the now conscience-stricken king and his guests... Before them passed, as in panoramic view, the deeds of their evil lives; they seemed to be arraigned before the judgment bar of the eternal God, whose power they had just defied. Where but a few moments before had been hilarity and blasphemous witticism, were pallid faces and cries of fear... Belshazzar was the most terrified of them all. He it was who above all others had been responsible for the rebellion against God which that night had reached its height in the Babylonian realm. In the presence of the unseen Watcher, the representative of Him whose power had been challenged and whose name had been blasphemed, the king was paralyzed with fear. *PK 524*

The Clear and Present Paraphrase

5. Suddenly, a hand appears out of nowhere and begins writing on the plaster right above the candlestick. Everyone at the party stares in unbelief.

6. Belshazzar's face turns ghastly pale with terror, his knees begin to buckle, and he starts profusely shaking.

7. The hand disappears, but the words that it wrote remain imprinted on the wall. Belshazzar sees the words; however, he is not able to determine what they mean. The king then begins yelling for his astrologers, fortune-tellers, and priests...anyone that can tell him what this message means. Once they arrive, Belshazzar says to them, "If anyone here can read the writing on this wall and tell me what it means, I will dress you in royal purple, and put a gold chain around your neck, and you will be the third most powerful man in the whole kingdom after my father and me."

KJV Bible	Daniel Commentary
8. Then came in all the king's wise *men*: but they could not read the writing, nor make known to the king the interpretation thereof.	**8. Then came in all** - The king's address recorded in vs. 7 was spoken to the wise men who were already present at the banquet when the handwriting appeared on the wall. Verse 8 would then apply to "all the king's wise men," including those who arrived at the banquet hall in response to Belshazzar's command. **They could not read** - Even though a reason is not provided, some scholars suggest the letters could not be read because of their dazzling brightness, or possibly they were only decipherable by divine revelation.
9. Then was king Belshazzar greatly troubled, and his countenance was changed in him, and his lords were astonied.	
10. *Now* the queen, by reason of the words of the king and his lords, came into the banquet house: *and* the queen spake and said, O king, live for ever: let not thy thoughts trouble thee, nor let thy countenance be changed:	
	10. The queen - Commentators have usually taken this "queen" to be the king's mother or grandmother.
11. There is a man in thy kingdom, in whom *is* the spirit of the holy gods; and in the days of thy father light and understanding and wisdom, like the wisdom of the gods, was found in him; whom the king Nebuchadnezzar thy father, the king, *I say*, thy father, made master of the magicians, astrologers, Chaldeans, *and* soothsayers;	**11. There is a man** - Daniel was not among the wise men summoned by the king as his term of public service had most likely ended some time ago. **The spirit of the holy gods** - Compare Nebuchadnezzar's statement (Daniel 4:8-9). This also furthers the suggested narrative that Daniel had not held office for some time, but the queen, a close relative of Nebuchadnezzar, was well acquainted with Daniel's legacy.

EG White Notes

In vain the king tried to read the burning letters. But here was a secret he could not fathom, a power he could neither understand nor gainsay. In despair he turned to the wise men of his realm for help. His wild cry rang out in the assembly, calling upon the astrologers, the Chaldeans, and the soothsayers to read the writing. Then the queen mother remembered Daniel, who, over half a century before, had made known to King Nebuchadnezzar the dream of the great image and its interpretation. *PK 527*

The Clear and Present Paraphrase

8. The rest of the wise men arrive and begin to examine the writing on the wall. However, none of them are able to make sense of the words written by the hand.

9. Once the king realizes that no one can read the message, it terrifies him even more to the point his face becomes pale like a dead man; this frightens everyone at the party.

10. The queen, who was made aware that something troubling was happening at the party, arrives at the banquet hall. After looking at the wall and seeing the terror on the face of Belshazzar and his guests, she turns to her son and says, "May Your Majesty live forever. There's no reason to be afraid or perplexed over this.

11. There's someone in Babylon in whom the spirit of the gods' live, and I'm confident he will be able to tell you what all of this means. When your grandfather was king, this man was found to have insight, understanding, and wisdom of the gods. Your grandfather placed him in charge of all the astrologers, fortune-tellers, and priests.

12. Forasmuch as an excellent spirit, and knowledge, and understanding, interpreting of dreams, and shewing of hard sentences, and dissolving of doubts, were found in the same Daniel, whom the king named Belteshazzar: now let Daniel be called, and he will shew the interpretation.

13. Then was Daniel brought in before the king. *And* the king spake and said unto Daniel, *Art* thou that Daniel, which *art* of the children of the captivity of Judah, whom the king my father brought out of Jewry?

14. I have even heard of thee, that the spirit of the gods *is* in thee, and *that* light and understanding and excellent wisdom is found in thee.

12. **Doubts** - Literally, "knots." The meaning seems to be "difficult tasks" or "problems" (RSV)

13. **Art thou that Daniel?** - This salutation suggests that Belshazzar was acquainted with Daniel's origin but had no official interaction with him. It is suggested that with Nebuchadnezzar's death, Daniel's belief system had come into disfavor with Babylon's current administration, and as a result, he was retired from public service.

14. **Spirit of the gods** - In contrast with the words of the queen (vs. 11) and of Nebuchadnezzar (Daniel 4:8), Belshazzar excludes the word "holy" in connection with the "gods."

EG White Notes

"Then was Daniel brought in before the king." Making an effort to regain his composure, Belshazzar said to the prophet: "Art thou that Daniel, which art of the children of the captivity of Judah, whom the king my father brought out of Jewry? *PK 528*

I have even heard of thee, that the spirit of the gods is in thee, and that light and understanding and excellent wisdom is found in thee. And now the wise men, the astrologers, have been brought in before me, that they should read this writing, and make known unto me the interpretation thereof: but they could not show the interpretation of the thing: and I have heard of thee, that thou canst make interpretations, and dissolve doubts... *PK 528*

The Clear and Present Paraphrase

12. Your grandfather did this because the spirit of the gods is in him. He has great insight and understanding; he can interpret dreams, solve riddles, and explain mysteries. His birth name is Daniel, but the king named him Belteshazzar. Summon him here, and he will be able to interpret the writing for you."

13. Belshazzar nods his head, and his guards bring Daniel before him. As Daniel stands in front of the king, Belshazzar says to him, "Are you the same Daniel that my grandfather Nebuchadnezzar brought to Babylon as a Jewish captive?" Daniel nods his head and responds, "Yes, I am."

14. Belshazzar continues, "I have heard that the spirit of the gods is in you, and you have great insight and understanding with the ability to interpret dreams, solve riddles, and explain mysteries."

15. And now the wise *men*, the astrologers, have been brought in before me, that they should read this writing, and make known unto me the interpretation thereof: but they could not shew the interpretation of the thing:

16. And I have heard of thee, that thou canst make interpretations, and dissolve doubts: now if thou canst read the writing, and make known to me the interpretation thereof, thou shalt be clothed with scarlet, and *have* a chain of gold about thy neck, and shalt be the third ruler in the kingdom.

17. Then Daniel answered and said before the king, Let thy gifts be to thyself, and give thy rewards to another; yet I will read the writing unto the king, and make known to him the interpretation.

16. **Doubts** - a knot (as tied up), i.e. (figuratively) a riddle.

17. **To thyself** - Some scholars believe Daniel declined the place of honor in order to avoid the appearance of self-interest. Other scholars suggest that Daniel, knowing the king's reign was about to end, had no interest in receiving favors from the man that just blasphemed the God of heaven.

...now if thou canst read the writing, and make known to me the interpretation thereof, thou shalt be clothed with scarlet, and have a chain of gold about thy neck, and shalt be the third ruler in the kingdom. *PK 528*

Before that terror-stricken throng, Daniel, unmoved by the promises of the king, stood in the quiet dignity of a servant of the Most High, not to speak words of flattery, but to interpret a message of doom. "Let thy gifts be to thyself," he said, "and give thy rewards to another; yet I will read the writing unto the king, and make known to him the interpretation." *PK 529*

15. Daniel attentively listens as Belshazzar points to the wall and says, "So, by now, I'm sure you've noticed that there are words written on that wall over there. I have no idea what they mean, which is the reason all my wise men, astrologers, and priests were brought in to read it, but unfortunately, they can't do it.

16. And that's why you're here, Daniel. I heard that you have the ability to interpret mysteries such as this. So here's what I'm going to do for you: If you can explain these words written on this wall over here, then I will place my royal purple on you, I'll put a chain around your neck, and you will be the third-highest ruler behind my father and me in the whole kingdom."

17. Daniel pauses for a moment, then responds to the king, "Your Majesty, I appreciate the offer, but I don't need any gifts for what I am about to tell you. I will read what it says, and then I will tell you what it means.

18. O thou king, the most high God gave Nebuchadnezzar thy father a kingdom, and majesty, and glory, and honour:

19. And for the majesty that he gave him, all people, nations, and languages, trembled and feared before him: whom he would he slew; and whom he would he kept alive; and whom he would he set up; and whom he would he put down.

20. But when his heart was lifted up, and his mind hardened in pride, he was deposed from his kingly throne, and they took his glory from him:

21. And he was driven from the sons of men; and his heart was made like the beasts, and his dwelling *was* with the wild asses: they fed him with grass like oxen, and his body was wet with the dew of heaven; till he knew that the most high God ruled in the kingdom of men, and *that* he appointeth over it whomsoever he will.

22. And thou his son, O Belshazzar, hast not humbled thine heart, though thou knewest all this;

18. **Nebuchadnezzar** - Here, Daniel reminds the king of what Nebuchadnezzar had experienced as a result of his refusal to fulfill the divine destiny regarding himself and the nation. Daniel attempted to show Belshazzar how evil his actions were toward God, the Lord of his life, and how he had not learned anything from his grandfather's experience.

19. **Majesty** – Greatness

20. **Lifted up** – Exalt

22. **His son** – Can also be translated as grandson.

EG White Notes

The prophet first reminded Belshazzar of matters with which he was familiar, but which had not taught him the lesson of humility that might have saved him. He spoke of Nebuchadnezzar's sin and fall, and of the Lord's dealings with him—the dominion and glory bestowed upon him, the divine judgment for his pride, and his subsequent acknowledgment of the power and mercy of the God of Israel; and then in bold and emphatic words he rebuked Belshazzar for his great wickedness. He held the king's sin up before him, showing him the lessons he might have learned but did not. Belshazzar had not read aright the experience of his grandfather, nor heeded the warning of events so significant to himself. The opportunity of knowing and obeying the true God had been given him, but had not been taken to heart, and he was about to reap the consequence of his rebellion.
PK 529

The Clear and Present Paraphrase

18. The Most High God made your grandfather, Nebuchadnezzar, the king. He also gave him majesty, glory, and great honor.

19. He was so great that people from all over the world feared him and trembled at his word. And Nebuchadnezzar did whatever he wanted to. He determined who lived and who died, or who was promoted or demoted...it was in his hands.

20. However, at some point, he became proud and arrogant, so he was removed from power.

21. He was driven from society. His mind was made like an animal. He ate grass like an ox and slept outside until he realized the Most High rules, and He alone appoints men as rulers over kingdoms.

22. King Belshazzar, you knew all of this, yet it didn't change your heart.

KJV Bible

23. But hast lifted up thyself against the Lord of heaven; and they have brought the vessels of his house before thee, and thou, and thy lords, thy wives, and thy concubines, have drunk wine in them; and thou hast praised the gods of silver, and gold, of brass, iron, wood, and stone, which see not, nor hear, nor know: and the God in whose hand thy breath *is*, and whose *are* all thy ways, hast thou not glorified:
24. Then was the part of the hand sent from him; and this writing was written.
25. And this *is* the writing that was written, MENE, MENE, TEKEL, UPHARSIN.

Daniel Commentary

23. **Thy breath** – The same breath that God allowed to sustain Belshazzar was the same breath the king used to insult God.
24. **This writing** - The inscription was still visible.
25. **This is the writing** - Daniel proceeds to read the words written on the wall, which most likely are four words in Aramaic. However, even after the words are read, it appears they still could not understand their meaning without divine enlightenment.

EG White Notes

Belshazzar...had had great opportunities of knowing the works of the living God, and His power, and of doing His will. He had been privileged with much light. His grandfather, Nebuchadnezzar, had been warned of his danger in forgetting God and glorifying himself. Belshazzar had a knowledge of his banishment from the society of men, and his association with the beasts of the field; and these facts, which ought to have been a lesson to him, he disregarded, as if they had never occurred; and he went on repeating the sins of his grandfather. He dared to commit the crimes which brought God's judgments upon Nebuchadnezzar. He was condemned, not alone that he himself was doing wickedly, but that he had not availed himself of opportunities and capabilities, if cultivated, of being right. *TM 436*

Turning to the Heaven-sent message on the wall, the prophet read, "Mene, Mene, Tekel, Upharsin." The hand that had traced the characters was no longer visible, but these four words were still gleaming forth with terrible distinctness; *PK 530*

The Clear and Present Paraphrase

23. Instead, you showed no respect for God. You took the cups from his holy temple in Jerusalem so you and your royal guests could drink from them while praising the gods of gold, silver, bronze, iron, wood, and stone. They aren't real, but the God of heaven, the One you mock, is the God who holds your very life and breath in his hands, and yet you totally insulted and disrespected him.

24. And this was the reason that God sent the hand that you saw writing on this wall.

25. So here is what it says: 'MENE, MENE, TEKEL, UPHARSIN.'

26. This *is* the interpretation of the thing: MENE; God hath numbered thy kingdom, and finished it.
27. TEKEL; Thou art weighed in the balances, and art found wanting.
28. PERES; Thy kingdom is divided, and given to the Medes and Persians.

26. **Mene** - An Aramaic word, meaning "numbered" or "counted." Daniel drew from this word the interpretation, "God hath numbered thy kingdom, and finished it." Some scholars believe this word was repeated for emphasis.
27. **Tekel** - *Teqil* comes from the verb "to weigh." Daniel informed the king as to the seriousness of this spiritual weighing as Belshazzar was found lacking in moral worth. **Found wanting** - Lacking
28. **Peres** - According to verse 25, "*upharsin*" was the word written on the wall, but here Daniel uses the word "peres" instead. Scholars note that *upharsin* means "pieces" or "divisions." Peres is the singular form of the word interpreted as "divided." Daniel, knowing that two nations were coming for Belshazzar, wanted to make it clear that it was only two pieces (one for Media, and the other for Persia), so he rendered the interpretation: "Thy kingdom is divided." He simplified it for Belshazzar so that he wouldn't be under the impression Babylon was to be broken into *upharsin* (*many* pieces) but rather *peres* (*two* pieces).

EG White Notes

Babylon was besieged by Cyrus, nephew of Darius the Mede, and commanding general of the combined armies of the Medes and Persians. *PK 523*

The Clear and Present Paraphrase

26. And this is what it means: MENE means that God has numbered the days of your kingdom, and they are coming to an end.
27. Tekel means that you have been examined by God, and the results of that examination are that you don't measure up to the standard that God has set for you.
28. Peres means that because you failed the examination, God is going to take this kingdom from you and divide it between the Medes and the Persians."

29. Then commanded Belshazzar, and they clothed Daniel with scarlet, and *put* a chain of gold about his neck, and made a proclamation concerning him, that he should be the third ruler in the kingdom.

30. In that night was Belshazzar the king of the Chaldeans slain.

31. And Darius the Median took the kingdom, *being* about threescore and two years old.

29. Then commanded Belshazzar - Daniel indicated he was not interested in the king's honors, but it may have been impossible to deter the king because of his drunken condition. Most likely, Daniel's "promotion" was only proclaimed among the nobles at the party and was not proclaimed in the streets due to their circumstances.

30. In the night - Some historians dispute the reign of Belshazzar as king, as his reign is not mentioned in the ancient writings found. However, ancient sources do confirm that King Nabonidus was absent from Babylon when it fell, while also confirming that "the impious king" of Babylon was slain when Cyrus attacked. No doubt this was Belshazzar.

31. Darius the Median - Not to be confused with Darius I (Ezra 4:5). This Darius only ruled for two years before he died. History has little to say about him, however, some believe he was also known as Cyaxares II.

EG White Notes

Even while he and his nobles were drinking from the sacred vessels of Jehovah, and praising their gods of silver and of gold, the Medes and the Persians, having turned the Euphrates out of its channel, were marching into the heart of the unguarded city. The army of Cyrus now stood under the walls of the palace; the city was filled with the soldiers of the enemy, "as with caterpillars" (verse 14); and their triumphant shouts could be heard above the despairing cries of the astonished revelers. "In that night was Belshazzar the king of the Chaldeans slain," and an alien monarch sat upon the throne. *PK 531*

This was the last feast of boasting held by the Chaldean king. He who bears long with the perversity of man passed the irrevocable sentence. Belshazzar had greatly dishonored Him who had exalted him as king, and his probation was taken from him. .... "In that night," the record says, "was Belshazzar the king of the Chaldeans slain. And Darius the Median took the kingdom." *Lt 51a, 1897*

The Clear and Present Paraphrase

29. Then, as Belshazzar promised, he orders Daniel to be dressed in royal purple and a has gold chain placed around his neck. Daniel's name is then proclaimed amongst the nobles as the third highest ruler in the kingdom.

30. However, that very night, the city is taken as Daniel prophesied it would. The Medes and Persians divert the Euphrates River, walk right into the city, take the guards by surprise, and kill Belshazzar.

31. And Darius the Mede, at sixty-two years old, takes the throne as the new ruler of Babylon.

DANIEL 5 - TEST YOUR KNOWLEDGE

1. What is the meaning of MENE, MENE, TEKEL, UPHARSIN? (*p. 110*)_____

   _____

2. True or False - Belshazzar was ignorant of Nebuchadnezzar's experiences with the God of heaven. (*pp. 106-107*)

3. True or False - Belshazzar was the son of King Nebuchadnezzar. (*p. 96*)

4. What did Belshazzar order to be brought to the party? (*p. 96*)_____

   _____

5. Why did Daniel replace the word *Peres* with the word *Upharsin* in his explanation of the handwriting on the wall? (*p. 110*)_____

   _____

6. What happened during the party that frightened Belshazzar? (*p. 98*)_____

   _____

7. What was happening outside the city gates while Belshazzar partied? (*p. 113*)

   _____

8. Who suggested that Daniel be summoned to interpret the writing on the wall? (*pp. 100-101*)_____

9. Belshazzar offered Daniel the third-highest position in the kingdom of Babylon. Who occupied the first two positions? (*p. 98*)_____

   _____

10. What was the name of the king who took the kingdom from Belshazzar? (*pp. 112-113*)_____

114

Questions for Discussion:

1. Was God more lenient with Nebuchadnezzar than Belshazzar?

2. If we look at Joseph and Daniel, these men were promoted, but never as a king or pharaoh. Is there a reason God didn't promote his servants to first in command?

3. Belshazzar seemed to exhibit the same prideful spirit as Nebuchadnezzar. Do you believe bad traits can be passed down to future generations? Name some examples from the Bible and from your personal life.

Daniel will face a tough decision. Should he obey God and lose his life? Or should he honor the king and lose his soul?

Daniel 6

Daniel in the Lion's Den

CHAPTER 6

1. It pleased Darius to set over the kingdom an hundred and twenty princes, which should be over the whole kingdom;
2. And over these three presidents; of whom Daniel *was* first: that the princes might give accounts unto them, and the king should have no damage.
3. Then this Daniel was preferred above the presidents and princes, because an excellent spirit *was* in him; and the king thought to set him over the whole realm.
4. Then the presidents and princes sought to find occasion against Daniel concerning the kingdom; but they could find none occasion nor fault; forasmuch as he *was* faithful, neither was there any error or fault found in him.

CHAPTER 6

1. **Princes** - Literally "satraps," which is a term used by some Greek historians for lower officials. The various details of the provincial administration of the Persian Empire before Darius I's reorganization are still unclear. Most likely, the number and size of his governors changed over the course of his reign.
2. **Daniel was first** - Literally, "Daniel was one." Daniel distinguished himself by diligent service. **No damage** - An organization was put in place to prevent loss of revenue and other potential damages.
3. **Excellent spirit** - A brief acquaintance with Daniel was ample proof to convince Darius that Daniel would be the best choice as chief administrator of the new empire.
4. **Any error** - Daniel, who was in his mid-eighties, was still able to perform his duties of state in such a way that no errors or faults could be charged against him. Clearly, this was due to his confidence in the guidance of the heavenly father and adherence to the laws of health.

CHAPTER 6

EG White Notes

The honors bestowed upon Daniel excited the jealousy of the leading men of the kingdom, and they sought for occasion of complaint against him. But they could find none, "forasmuch as he was faithful, neither was there any error or fault found in him." *PK 539*

CHAPTER 6

The Clear and Present Paraphrase

1. After taking the Babylonian throne, Darius divides the country into one hundred and twenty provinces and appoints governors over each of those provinces.

2. He also appoints three more officials (Daniel being one of them) as overseers of the governors.

3. Once again, Daniel proved to be so much more excellent than any of Darius' government officials that Darius considers placing Daniel in charge of the whole kingdom!

4. Some of the officials within the government take notice of this, and jealousy begins to manifest itself among them. So they formulate a plan. They decide to find some fault with Daniel...some kind of negligence on his part, in order to take him down.

   However, after observing Daniel for some time, they begin to realize they can't find a single neglect on his part!

5. Then said these men, We shall not find any occasion against this Daniel, except we find *it* against him concerning the law of his God.
6. Then these presidents and princes assembled together to the king, and said thus unto him, King Darius, live for ever.
7. All the presidents of the kingdom, the governors, and the princes, the counsellors, and the captains, have consulted together to establish a royal statute, and to make a firm decree, that whosoever shall ask a petition of any God or man for thirty days, save of thee, O king, he shall be cast into the den of lions.

5. **The law of his God** - Undoubtedly, Daniel's enemies noticed that he was absent from his office every Sabbath.
6. **These presidents and princes** - Only the particular governors who envied Daniel probably appeared before the king.
7. **All** - This is probably a lie, for it is questionable that all were consulted. **Whosoever shall ask a petition** - Some scholars believe that the Medes showed far less religious tolerance than the Persians. **Den of lions** - Although no examples of capital punishment by throwing the culprit before wild animals are known from contemporary records in Persian times, these sources do speak of extraordinarily barbaric forms of capital punishment (SDA Bible Commentary Vol 4 pg. 811-812).

EG White Notes

Thereupon the presidents and princes, counseling together, devised a scheme whereby they hoped to accomplish the prophet's destruction. They determined to ask the king to sign a decree which they should prepare, forbidding any person in the realm to ask anything of God or man, except of Darius the king, for the space of thirty days. A violation of this decree should be punished by casting the offender into a den of lions. *PK 540*

The Clear and Present Paraphrase

5. In desperation, the conspirators call a secret meeting. They knew that Darius would eventually put Daniel in charge of the whole kingdom if they didn't find something wrong with the Hebrew. So the conspirators come up with a devious plan: "Men," they begin, "If we can't find anything wrong with his work, then we will find something wrong with his religion!"

6. Everyone begins to smile because they know Daniel will be more loyal to his God than he will be to the king. And so they make their way to see Darius. They enter his presence and greet him with the usual salutation, saying, "May Your Majesty live forever!"

7. One of the conspirators speaks up and says, "Your Majesty, as your presidents, governors, counselors, and officials, we believe everyone's loyalty should be tested." King Darius sits up in his chair. "We believe," he continues, "that everyone should be tested to see if they are loyal to you. If anyone fails this test, they don't deserve the privilege of your rulership, and that individual should be thrown into the lion's den.

8. Now, O king, establish the decree, and sign the writing, that it be not changed, according to the law of the Medes and Persians, which altereth not.
9. Wherefore king Darius signed the writing and the decree.
10. Now when Daniel knew that the writing was signed, he went into his house; and his windows being open in his chamber toward Jerusalem, he kneeled upon his knees three times a day, and prayed, and gave thanks before his God, as he did aforetime.
11. Then these men assembled, and found Daniel praying and making supplication before his God.

8. **It be not changed** – Regarding the irreversibility of the Medo-Persian law compare Esther 1:19; 8:8. **Medes and Persians** - Since Darius was a "Mede," it is only natural that any member of his court referring to the law of the land would speak of "the law of the Medes and Persians."
10. **He kneeled** - The Bible notes various postures for prayer. The most common attitude in prayer seems to have been that of kneeling. **Three times a day** - In later Jewish tradition, the offering of prayer three times a day took place at the third, sixth, and ninth hours of the day (the hours being counted from sunrise). This custom of the three daily times of prayer also seems to have been adopted in the early Christian Church.
11. **Found Daniel praying** - The plotters didn't have to wait long in order to see Daniel disregard the king's decree. No matter the cost, Daniel felt that he should continue his regular prayer habits.

EG White Notes

The king's vanity was flattered. Not for a moment did he think that Daniel, his beloved and honored servant, would in any way be affected by the law. He signed the decree, and with it in their possession, the presidents and princes went forth from his presence, evil triumph depicted on their countenances. They deemed that the man they hated was now in their power. *YI November 1, 1900*

Daniel heard of what had been done, but he made no protest. He could see the design of his enemies. He knew that they would watch closely his going out and his coming in, but he calmly attended to his duties, and at the hour of prayer he went to his chamber, and kneeling by the open window, with his face toward Jerusalem, he prayed to his God.

Some may ask, Why did not Daniel lift his soul to God in secret prayer? Would not the Lord, knowing the situation, have excused his servant from kneeling openly before him? Or why did he not kneel before God in some secret place, where his enemies could not see him? *YI November 1, 1900*

The Clear and Present Paraphrase

8. To make this happen, all you need to do is sign this document, and this decree officially becomes part of the unchangeable Medo-Persian law."

9. Darius briefly looks at the document, then places his royal seal on it. The decree has officially been added to the law of the land.

10. Daniel, not long afterward, is informed of this new law. However, this doesn't change Daniel's routine. Knowing that what he is about to do is now considered breaking the law, Daniel still goes to his rooftop, opens his window, and prays toward Jerusalem as he has customarily done three times a day.

11. However, this time, he is being watched. The conspirators knew Daniel's routine, so they simply watched and waited for Daniel. Their plan paid off, and now they have the evidence they need to get rid of Daniel once and for all!

12. Then they came near, and spake before the king concerning the king's decree; Hast thou not signed a decree, that every man that shall ask *a petition* of any God or man within thirty days, save of thee, O king, shall be cast into the den of lions? The king answered and said, The thing *is* true, according to the law of the Medes and Persians, which altereth not.

13. Then answered they and said before the king, That Daniel, which *is* of the children of the captivity of Judah, regardeth not thee, O king, nor the decree that thou hast signed, but maketh his petition three times a day.

14. Then the king, when he heard *these* words, was sore displeased with himself, and set *his* heart on Daniel to deliver him: and he laboured till the going down of the sun to deliver him.

13. Of the captivity - These men did not even respect his office but characterized him merely as a foreigner, a Jewish exile. Essentially, the men were saying to the king—How could a man whom the king had so highly honored be so brazen as to defy the royal orders openly? Their words were calculated to lead Darius to regard Daniel as ungrateful, if not traitorous.

14. Deliver him - Darius suddenly realized that the whole matter had been concocted, not as he had thought, to bring honor to his reign and person, but to deprive him of a true friend and trustworthy public servant. Despite all his efforts, the king couldn't find any legal loophole by which to save Daniel and at the same time preserve the basic Median and Persian law.

EG White Notes

The next morning they laid their complaint before the king. Daniel, his most honored and faithful statesman, had set the royal decree at defiance. "Hast thou not signed a decree," they reminded him, "that every man that shall ask a petition of any god or man within thirty days, save of thee, O king, shall be cast into the den of lions?" "The thing is true," the king answered, "according to the law of the Medes and Persians, which altereth not."

Exultantly they now informed Darius of the conduct of his most trusted adviser. "That Daniel, which is of the children of the captivity of Judah," they exclaimed, "regardeth not thee, O king, nor the decree that thou hast signed, but maketh his petition three times a day."

When the monarch heard these words, he saw at once the snare that had been set for his faithful servant. He saw that it was not zeal for kingly glory and honor, but jealousy against Daniel, that had led to the proposal for a royal decree. *PK 542-543*

The Clear and Present Paraphrase

12. The men hastily make their way to the king. As they stand in front of Darius, they begin their rehearsed opening statement. "Your Majesty," they begin, "didn't you sign a decree that for thirty days no one can pray to any god or man except you? And if that decree is broken, that man or woman is to be thrown into the lion's den?" King Darius confidently responds to the inquiry, "Absolutely!" He continues, "And this is officially part of the Median and Persian law, so I can't even change it."

13. The conversation is going according to plan. The men then respond to the king, "Your Majesty, you know that captured Jew named Daniel? Well, he is ignoring the law and continues praying to his God."

14. Darius slowly sits back in his chair. He now realizes that this whole time, these men were simply out to get Daniel, and they used his power, his throne, and his name to do it. After the men left, King Darius spent all day trying to find a way to save Daniel.

15. Then these men assembled unto the king, and said unto the king, Know, O king, that the law of the Medes and Persians *is*, That no decree nor statute which the king establisheth may be changed.
16. Then the king commanded, and they brought Daniel, and cast *him* into the den of lions. *Now* the king spake and said unto Daniel, Thy God whom thou servest continually, he will deliver thee.
17. And a stone was brought, and laid upon the mouth of the den; and the king sealed it with his own signet, and with the signet of his lords; that the purpose might not be changed concerning Daniel.

15. **Assembled** - The men knew they had a legal right to demand Daniel's execution and that there was no loophole in the law by which he could escape.
16. **Deliver thee** - The words of Darius give us some indication that Darius may have been familiar with the miracles that God had performed in the days of Nebuchadnezzar and Belshazzar.
17. **A stone was brought** - We have yet to discover an ancient lion's den; therefore, it's impossible to reconstruct an accurate picture of such a place. **Sealed it** - The official sealing by the king and his lords had a twofold purpose: It served as a guarantee to the king that Daniel would not be killed by any other means, in case he was not harmed by the lions. On the other hand, the seal provided assurance to Daniel's enemies that no attempt could be made to save him, in the event he was not immediately torn to pieces by the wild animals.

Daniel was brought before the king and his princes to answer the accusation brought against him. He had opportunity to speak for himself, and he boldly acknowledged his belief in the living God, the maker of heaven and earth. He made a noble confession of faith, relating his experience from his first connection with the kingdom. In his perplexity and distress, Darius said to Daniel, I have done all I can to save you. I can do no more. "Thy God, whom thou servest continually, he will deliver thee," he added, as he bade him a sorrowful farewell. *YI November 1, 1900*

"Then the king commanded, and they brought Daniel, and cast him into the den of lions... A stone was laid on the mouth of the den, and the king himself "sealed it with his own signet, and with the signet of his lords; that the purpose might not be changed concerning Daniel. *PK 543*

15. Time has passed. The sun has set, and the men have now returned to remind Darius of their earlier conversation. "Your Majesty," they begin, "we just wanted to remind you, in case you forgot, that you can't change this law. There is nothing that you can do here."

16. Darius reluctantly gives in and sentences Daniel to death. As the guards bring Daniel to his place of punishment, King Darius and his princes meet him there. The guards bring Daniel to King Darius as the king is desirous of having one last conversation with his friend. With tears in his eyes, he says to Daniel, "I have no choice but to carry out this sentence...and...I don't know what tomorrow holds, but what I do know is that you've been faithful in serving your God, and if He is what you say He is, then I truly believe that He will rescue you from these lions."

17. After this, they lower Daniel into the lions' den, roll a huge boulder over the entrance and put sealer all around the boulder. This is done so no one can break the seal and rescue Daniel or even kill him should the lions fail to do so.

KJV Bible

18. Then the king went to his palace, and passed the night fasting: neither were instruments of musick brought before him: and his sleep went from him.

19. Then the king arose very early in the morning, and went in haste unto the den of lions.

20. And when he came to the den, he cried with a lamentable voice unto Daniel: *and* the king spake and said to Daniel, O Daniel, servant of the living God, is thy God, whom thou servest continually, able to deliver thee from the lions?

Daniel Commentary

18. **Instruments of musick** - Aramaic *dachawan*. The word is obscure. There are many other interpretations of this word, ranging from tables, foods, musicians, dancing women, musical instruments, perfumes, and entertainers.

19. **Very early in the morning** - Aramaic *shepharpar*, meaning "dawn."

20. **Lamentable** - Aramaic *'asib*, "sad," "pained," full of anxiety." The dreadful experience of seeing his most faithful servant thrown to the lions was followed by a long, sleepless night. **Servant of the living God** - These words reveal a level of acquaintance with the God and religion of Daniel. The fact that the king referred to the God of Daniel as "The living God" implies that Daniel probably instructed him concerning the nature and power of Jehovah.

EG White Notes

Then the king went to his palace, and passed the night fasting: neither were instruments of music brought before him: and his sleep went from him." God did not prevent Daniel's enemies from casting him into the lions' den; He permitted evil angels and wicked men thus far to accomplish their purpose; but it was that He might make the deliverance of His servant more marked, and the defeat of the enemies of truth and righteousness. *PK 543*

Early the next morning, hoping and yet despairing, condemning himself, and praying to him whom he began to recognize as the true God...*YI November 1, 1900*

"O Daniel, servant of the living God, is thy God, whom thou servest continually, able to deliver thee from the lions?" *PK 544*

The Clear and Present Paraphrase

18. King Darius returns to his palace, but he's so distraught that he can't eat his dinner and has no desire for his usual evening amusements. This is because all he can do is think about Daniel. The king goes to bed, but he can't sleep. So he stays up all night worrying about Daniel.

19. As soon as morning arrives, King Darius gets dressed and hurries to the lion's den to see if Daniel survived. He wonders if Daniel's God has been able to protect him.

20. As King Darius arrives at the last known spot he saw Daniel alive, he anxiously calls out, "Daniel! Servant of the Most High God! Has your God delivered you?"

21. Then said Daniel unto the king, O king, live for ever.
22. My God hath sent his angel, and hath shut the lions' mouths, that they have not hurt me: forasmuch as before him innocency was found in me; and also before thee, O king, have I done no hurt.
23. Then was the king exceeding glad for him, and commanded that they should take Daniel up out of the den. So Daniel was taken up out of the den, and no manner of hurt was found upon him, because he believed in his God.

21. **O king, live for ever** - See on chapter 2:4 for this ceremonial greeting
22. **Shut the lions' mouths** - The writer of Hebrews, when speaking about faith, refers to this particular experience of Daniel (Hebrews 11:33). **Innocency was found in me** - Daniel, up to this point, had not defended himself or his actions before being thrown into the lion's den. Any word spoken at that time might have been seen by his accusers as weakness or fear, or worse—regret for obeying God. However, after the ordeal was over, Daniel saw fit to declare his innocence.
23. **Take Daniel up** - The requirements of the royal judgment had been met. The decree did not require that Daniel die in the lion's den but only that he "be cast into the den of lions." And now that the requirement was met, there were no constitutional restrictions to prevent the king from removing his friend from the lions' den.

EG White Notes

The voice of the prophet replied: "O king, live forever. My God hath sent His angel, and hath shut the lions' mouths, that they have not hurt me: forasmuch as before Him innocency was found in me; and also before thee, O king, have I done no hurt.

"Then was the king exceeding glad for him, and commanded that they should take Daniel up out of the den. So Daniel was taken up out of the den, and no manner of hurt was found upon him, because he believed in his God. *PK 544*

The Clear and Present Paraphrase

21. For a moment, the king hears silence. Then a familiar voice is heard from the lions' den. "Your Majesty," Daniel begins, "may you live forever!

22. My God sent his angel and took away their desire to eat me so that they didn't even touch me! My God did this because he knew that I was innocent and that I have been loyal to you all this time."

23. King Darius, unable to hide his excitement at hearing Daniel's voice, quickly orders his guards to throw a rope to Daniel and pull him out of the lion's den. When he lifts up Daniel, everyone is shocked to see that there's not even a scratch on him! There is only one reason for this miracle: Daniel trusted in his God.

24. And the king commanded, and they brought those men which had accused Daniel, and they cast *them* into the den of lions, them, their children, and their wives; and the lions had the mastery of them, and brake all their bones in pieces or ever they came at the bottom of the den.

25. Then king Darius wrote unto all people, nations, and languages, that dwell in all the earth; Peace be multiplied unto you.

26. I make a decree, That in every dominion of my kingdom men tremble and fear before the God of Daniel: for he *is* the living God, and stedfast for ever, and his kingdom *that* which shall not be destroyed, and his dominion *shall be even* unto the end.

24. **They cast them** - Some critics have attempted to show that this story is unhistorical by claiming that the den in which the lions were kept could not have been large enough to receive 122 men along with their wives and children; furthermore, they don't believe there could have been enough lions in Babylon to eat so many people. However, these critics are assuming that all 120 princes and the two presidents of verses 1 and 2 were involved in the unfortunate experience. One must keep in mind that the Bible doesn't state 122 people were the number condemned to death.
Their children - This sentence was of typical fashion of dictators of that era.

26. **I make a decree** - There is no need to conclude that the king personally departed from the Pagan religion of the Medes. Darius simply acknowledged the God of Daniel as the true living God, whose kingdom and dominion are everlasting. However, it has been noted that the king did not acknowledge Daniel's God as the *only* true God.

EG White Notes

"And the king commanded, and they brought those men which had accused Daniel, and they cast them into the den of lions, them, their children, and their wives; and the lions had the mastery of them, and brake all their bones in pieces or ever they came at the bottom of the den."

Once more a proclamation was issued by a heathen ruler, exalting the God of Daniel as the true God. "King Darius wrote unto all people, nations, and languages, that dwell in all the earth; Peace be multiplied unto you. I make a decree, that in every dominion of my kingdom men tremble and fear before the God of Daniel: for He is the living God, and steadfast forever, and His kingdom that which shall not be destroyed, and His dominion shall be even unto the end. *PK 544-545*

The Clear and Present Paraphrase

24. After this, King Darius orders those who conspired against Daniel to be thrown into the lion's den along with their wives and children. Unfortunately for them, Daniel's angel had already left, and the lion's appetites returned. This becomes painfully evident as the lions begin mauling and tearing them apart while they are being lowered into the den...even before their feet touch the ground!

25. After Daniel's enemies were all placed in the lion's den, the king makes the following announcement to everyone in his kingdom: "Peace to every one of you!

26. I am making a decree that throughout my kingdom, men and women should show respect for the God of Daniel. His God is the living God and will be so forever. His kingdom will never be destroyed, and His dominion will last forever."

27. He delivereth and rescueth, and he worketh signs and wonders in heaven and in earth, who hath delivered Daniel from the power of the lions.
28. So this Daniel prospered in the reign of Darius, and in the reign of Cyrus the Persian.

28. **In the reign** - The fact that these words are repeated does not signify a separation of the Persian kingdom from the Median, but simply a distinction of rulers, one being a Mede and the other a Persian. The way the sentence is constructed allows interpretations that make Cyrus either a co-ruler with Darius or the successor to Darius.

EG White Notes

He delivereth and rescueth, and He worketh signs and wonders in heaven and in earth, who hath delivered Daniel from the power of the lions."

The wicked opposition to God's servant was now completely broken. "Daniel prospered in the reign of Darius, and in the reign of Cyrus the Persian." And through association with him, these heathen monarchs were constrained to acknowledge his God as "the living God, and steadfast forever, and His kingdom that which shall not be destroyed." *PK 545*

The Clear and Present Paraphrase

27. I am a witness that He is able to save anyone He wants, and He performs miracles in heaven and on earth. This is the God who took away the lion's appetites and saved Daniel, His servant."

28. Daniel gets restored to his position and faithfully serves Darius until the Median king's death. Afterward, Daniel serves King Cyrus and is just as prosperous under Cyrus as he was under Darius.

DANIEL 6 - TEST YOUR KNOWLEDGE

1. What proclamation was made by Darius after Daniel was freed from the lion's den? (*p. 132*)_____

2. How many princes did Darius set over the Kingdom of Babylon? (*pp. 118-119*)_____

3. Why was the lion's den sealed? (*p. 126*)_____

4. Why was Daniel preferred over the other princes? (*p. 118*)_____
   _____

5. What did Darius attempt to do once he realized Daniel would have to die? (*pp. 124-125*)_____

6. Why did the princes attempt to use God's law against Daniel? (*p. 119*)_____
   _____

7. How many times per day did Daniel have prayer? (*p. 122*)_____

8. Why didn't Darius change the law in favor of Daniel? (*p. 122*)_____
   _____

9. What did Daniel say to Darius to proclaim his innocence? (*p. 130*)_____
   _____

10. How were the princes that tried to destroy Daniel punished? (*p. 132*)_____
    _____

Questions for Discussion:

1. Does the spirit of jealousy, exhibited by the princes, remind you of another being who was jealous of Christ?

2. If you were living during Old Testament times, would you be nervous if you were related to someone of nobility?

3. Daniel exhibited a spirit of excellence and loyalty to God at all times. How should we relate to Daniel in our daily lives?

4. Why didn't Daniel simply pray in private to avoid this whole situation?

Daniel, once again, is shown the world's empires, but this time it's not a statue of metals, it's a group of wild animals. These wild animals reveal the future of the world.

Daniel 7

The Animalistic Attributes of the Four Kingdoms

CHAPTER 7

1. In the first year of Belshazzar king of Babylon Daniel had a dream and visions of his head upon his bed: then he wrote the dream, *and* told the sum of the matters.
2. Daniel spake and said, I saw in my vision by night, and, behold, the four winds of the heaven strove upon the great sea.
3. And four great beasts came up from the sea, diverse one from another.

CHAPTER 7

1. **First year of Belshazzar** - Please note, the events of chapters 5 & 6 took place after those recorded in the 7th chapter. **Had a dream** - The prophecy of chapter 7 covers the same span of history as the dream of chapter 2. **Sum of the matters** - The important details.
2. **Winds** - These four winds represent movements of strife that could be diplomatic, warlike, political, or otherwise, coming from north, south, east, and west that were to shape the history of that period. **Strove** - "To stir up." This represents continued action. **Great sea** - The sea here is symbolic of the nations of the world (See Revelation 17:15).
3. **Four...beasts** – Can represent kings (vs. 17) or kingdoms (vs. 23). There is a general consensus that these four beasts represent the same world powers symbolized by the image in chapter 2. **Came up** - These world powers represented did not bear rulership at the same time but successively. **Diverse** - The diversity here is consistent with the diversity of metals present in the image of chapter 2.

CHAPTER 7

Shortly before the fall of Babylon, when Daniel was meditating on these prophecies and seeking God for an understanding of the times, a series of visions was given him concerning the rise and fall of kingdoms. With the first vision, as recorded in the seventh chapter of the book of Daniel, an interpretation was given; yet not all was made clear to the prophet. *PK 553*

The great kingdoms that have ruled the world were presented to the prophet Daniel as beasts of prey, rising when the "four winds of the heaven strove upon the great sea." [Daniel 7:2.] In Revelation 17, an angel explained that waters represent "peoples, and multitudes, and nations, and tongues." [Revelation 17:15.] Winds are a symbol of strife. The four winds of heaven striving upon the great sea, represent the terrible scenes of conquest and revolution by which kingdoms have attained to power. *1888 GC 440*

CHAPTER 7

1. Let's go back a few years and revisit the first year of Belshazzar's reign. At that time, God gave me visions and dreams, in which I kept a record of what was shown to me. Here are the important details of what God revealed:

2. One vision, in particular, happened at night. What I saw were peoples, multitudes, nations, and kingdoms from every direction of the known world being stirred up with the spirit of war. I also saw that there would be revolutions and conquests in order for these kingdoms to obtain more power.

3. Then the Lord showed me four animals representing four empires that would ultimately dominate the world through these wars of conquest. Not simultaneously, but one after another, they were to arise among the peoples, multitudes, nations, and kingdoms and have dominion over the known world. While these four world powers were all part of the same vision, they all had unique qualities that made them different from each other.

KJV Bible

4. The first *was* like a lion, and had eagle's wings: I beheld till the wings thereof were plucked, and it was lifted up from the earth, and made stand upon the feet as a man, and a man's heart was given to it.
5. And behold another beast, a second, like to a bear, and it raised up itself on one side, and *it had* three ribs in the mouth of it between the teeth of it: and they said thus unto it, Arise, devour much flesh.

Daniel Commentary

4. **Lion...eagle's wings** - The lion as the king of beasts and the eagle as the king of birds fittingly represented the empire of Babylon. The winged lion is found on Babylonian objects of art. **Plucked** - This likely refers to the time when less powerful rulers ruled the kingdom of Babylon, and the kingdom lost its power and glory. Some scholars suggest this may refer to the time Nebuchadnezzar lost his reason for seven years. **Lifted up** - A lion standing upright is indicative of the loss of lion-like qualities. **A man's heart** - A "man-hearted" lion represents a kingdom that became weak.
5. **Bear** - The Persian, or Medo-Persian Empire. As silver is inferior to gold, so is the bear inferior to the lion. **On one side** - Of the two parts of the kingdom (Media and Persia), the latter would one day become the dominant power, or rather the "raised up" power. **Three ribs** - Media and or Persia was directly involved in the destruction of the three world empires that preceded it. (Egypt, Assyria, and Babylon).

EG White Notes

Every nation that has come on the stage of action has been permitted to occupy its place on the earth that it might be seen whether it would fulfill the purpose of "the Watcher and the Holy One." Prophecy has traced the rise and fall of the world's great empires—Babylon, Medo-Persia, Greece, and Rome. With each of these, as with nations of less power, history repeated itself. Each had its period of test. Each failed. Its glory faded, its power departed, and its place was occupied by another. *True Education 106*

The Clear and Present Paraphrase

4. The first kingdom, presented as a lion, was Babylon. What makes Babylon unique is that, just as the lion is the king of the jungle, Babylon will be considered the most glorious out of all the kingdoms that follow it. And the manner it conquered and spread itself throughout the region was like no other as it overpowered the known world. However, God will only allow Babylon to rule for so long; eventually, He is going to humble this nation, and its reign will be over.

5. Then I was shown the next world power to come up among the peoples, multitudes, nations, and kingdoms of the known world will be Medo-Persia. This nation was presented to me as a bear. And just as a bear is considered inferior to a lion, Medo-Persia will be less glorious than Babylon. Then I noticed that the bear was raised up on one side, which revealed that Persia would one day conquer Media. I also noticed the bear had three ribs in its mouth representing Egypt, Assyria, and Babylon—the three world powers it subdued. God will permit Medo-Persia to dominate all other nations.

6. After this I beheld, and lo another, like a leopard, which had upon the back of it four wings of a fowl; the beast had also four heads; and dominion was given to it.

6. **Like a leopard** - The leopard is known for its swiftness and agility in its movements. The power succeeding the Persian Empire is identified in chapter 8:21 as "Grecia" under Alexander the Great. In 323 BC, he died from, as some believe, malaria. **Four wings of a fowl** - The leopard by itself is swift enough, but this speed is compounded with the addition of four wings. This describes the amazing speed of Alexander's conquests. **Four heads** – Without a clear successor, the Greek Empire fell into civil war after Alexander's death. Once the smoke cleared, Greek was divided into four kingdoms ruled by four of Alexander's generals. The four heads are symbolic of the kingdoms that Alexander's former generals established.

- Lysimachus ruled Asia Minor (North)
- Ptolemy ruled Egypt (South)
- Seleucus ruled Syria and the nations toward the East.
- Cassander ruled Macedonia (West)

EG White Notes

Alexander found it much easier to subdue kingdoms than to rule his own spirit. After conquering nations, he fell through the indulgence of appetite,—the victim of intemperance. *ST March 19, 1902*

The Clear and Present Paraphrase

6. After this, God showed me the next world empire that would rise to power would be the Greek Empire. God presented this kingdom to me as a leopard with four wings and four heads. God used wings to emphasize how quickly this Empire will conquer the known world. It will achieve world dominion faster than all its predecessors, but eventually, this kingdom will end up being divided into four separate nations toward the north, south, east, and west, which is why the leopard was presented with four heads.

7. After this I saw in the night visions, and behold a fourth beast, dreadful and terrible, and strong exceedingly; and it had great iron teeth: it devoured and brake in pieces, and stamped the residue with the feet of it: and it *was* diverse from all the beasts that *were* before it; and it had ten horns.

7. **Fourth beast** - It is clear from history that the world power succeeding the third empire was Rome. There is no date for this succession as its dominance was a gradual process. However, Rome's transition to a world power was evident once it absorbed the remaining territories of the divided Greek Empire. **Great iron teeth** - Rome devoured nations and peoples in its conquests. **Stamped the residue** – This represents absolute annihilation. Rome was merciless. Where this nation did not destroy a people, it made them slaves. **Ten horns** - A horn is the symbol the Bible uses to represent a line of kings for any given nation. It appears that the ten horns on the terrible Beast represent the lineage of kings who successively ruled the world prior to Rome's dominance. In essence, Rome contained components of all the world powers that preceded it.

EG White Notes

While the nations rejected God's principles, and in this rejection ruined themselves, it was still seen that the divine, overruling purpose was working through all their movements.
True Education 106

The Clear and Present Paraphrase

7. As these Greek nations declined from internal strife, I saw the fourth Beast that symbolizes the fourth world power. However, this time, the animal that God chose to represent this empire was unlike anything I had ever seen! All I know was that this animal was extremely frightening! It was very strong, with great iron teeth, and it used those teeth to devour everything in its path. This was the animal that God chose to represent the last world power! God was letting us know that this nation will not only dominate the known world, but it will crush and devour any nation in its path. This Beast was very different from all the other Beasts in a number of ways. To begin with, this creature had ten horns which represented ten lines of kings.

8\. I considered the horns, and, behold, there came up among them another little horn, before whom there were three of the first horns plucked up by the roots: and, behold, in this horn *were* eyes like the eyes of man, and a mouth speaking great things

8\. **Little Horn** - This entity represents all the kings who ruled Pagan Rome and all the Popes who had authority in Papal Rome. **Before** - "in the presence of." Even though the Little Horn's main identity is the Papacy, the prophecy appears to present the Papacy as if it were the power that conquered the divided Greek territories. In this manner, we see that the Little Horn represents the Roman kings and Popes. **Three of the first horns** - As Rome rose to world dominance, it began conquering the divided territories of the Greek Empire. According to the angel, the Little Horn would ultimately destroy three of the ten kingships. **Plucked up by the roots** – These three kingships were destroyed by the Roman Empire. **Eyes of man** - Proverbs 27:20 says, "...the eyes of man are never satisfied." The Papacy's insatiable appetite for power and control led it to assume the prerogatives that only belong to Christ. **Mouth speaking great things** – The voice given to the Papacy was often used by the Popes to boast of their infallibility and the decrees they enacted that superseded the Word of God.

EG White Notes

This symbol, as most Protestants have believed, represents the papacy, which succeeded to the power and seat and authority once held by the Roman empire. *From Here to Forever 271*

The Clear and Present Paraphrase

8. While I was watching these horns that represented ten kingships, I saw another horn rise up among them, but this horn was significantly smaller than the others. I would later understand that this Little Horn represented all the kings of the Roman Empire, which will begin as a small city in Italy. This horn will later transition from symbolizing kings to symbolizing the Popes that will rule during the Empire's Papal phase. I then watched as the Little Horn destroyed three of the ten horns that had arisen. This was an indication that Rome's rise to dominance would only occur after it conquered the nations ruled by these three existing kingships. I also saw that these kings and Popes would never be satisfied and would continue seeking for more riches, power, and glory—even to the point of making blasphemous claims against God and His Church.

9. I beheld till the thrones were cast down, and the Ancient of days did sit, whose garment *was* white as snow, and the hair of his head like the pure wool: his throne *was like* the fiery flame, *and* his wheels *as* burning fire.

10. A fiery stream issued and came forth from before him: thousand thousands ministered unto him, and ten thousand times ten thousand stood before him: the judgment was set, and the books were opened.

9. **Cast down** - "to place," or "to set up," though it may also mean, "to throw." A symbolic representation of the great final courtroom. **Ancient of days** - In the original language, this phrase can be interpreted as "The One Who Is Older Than Time" or "The One Who Was Worshipped Since The Beginning Of Time." This phrase obviously refers to God Almighty. **Whose garment** - Since no man hath seen God (John 1:18), we can be certain Daniel only saw a representation of the Deity. The extent of this representation is unknown.

10. **Thousand thousands** - These represent the heavenly angels. **Judgment was set** - It's almost as if Daniel witnessed a blending of the Investigative Judgment right before Jesus comes and the climax of the executive judgment right before hellfire destroys the wicked. **The books were opened** - We are not told what books these were, but no doubt, one of the books was the Book of Life (Revelation 20:12). The other book was possibly the Book of Remembrance (Malachi 3:16).

EG White Notes

Thus was presented to the prophet's vision the great and solemn day when the characters and the lives of men should pass in review before the Judge of all the earth, and to every man should be rendered "according to his works." The Ancient of days is God the Father. *GC 479*

These things are soon to come to pass. When? When? "He that is unjust, let him be unjust still, and he which is filthy, let him be filthy still: and he that is righteous, let him be righteous still: and he that is holy, let him be holy still." [Revelation 22:11.] This decision is passed in heaven before Christ shall come. *LT 101, 1896*

The Revelator, describing the same scene, adds, "Another book was opened, which is the book of life; and the dead were judged out of those things which were written in the books, according to their works." [Revelation 20:12.] *GC 480*

The Clear and Present Paraphrase

9. I continued watching till I saw thrones being set up, and The One, who precedes time, sat down. His robe was as white as snow, and His hair was white like wool. His throne and the wheels of His throne were literally on fire!

10. Then a stream of fire shot out from His throne. Thousands and thousands of angels attended to Him, and it looked like tens of thousands multiplied by tens of thousands of angels stood before Him, ready to serve Him. In vision, I was witnessing the beginning and the culmination of the great and final judgment that was set to take place at the end of the world. The Books were opened, and the lives of men passed in review before God.

KJV Bible	Daniel Commentary
11. I beheld then because of the voice of the great words which the horn spake: I beheld *even* till the beast was slain, and his body destroyed, and given to the burning flame. 12. As concerning the rest of the beasts, they had their dominion taken away: yet their lives were prolonged for a season and time. 13. I saw in the night visions, and, behold, *one* like the Son of man came with the clouds of heaven, and came to the Ancient of days, and they brought him near before him.	11. **I beheld** - This clause introduces the transition to the next scene. **Great words** - See vs. 25. **Was slain** - This represents the end of the Little Horn's system or organization. 12. **Dominion taken away** – The previous world powers had all fallen; however, spiritually, they continued to live through the ten kingships, even though they had no dominion during Rome's supremacy (see Revelation 17:12). 13. **Like the Son of man** - "Like a son of man." The translation, "One, human in form," would more adequately represent the Aramaic phrase. The Son of God is introduced literally as "One, of human form." **Came to the Ancient of days** - This cannot be the Second Coming, as Christ, in this scripture, is seen as coming to His Father, not to the earth. This represents the investigative judgment.

EG White Notes

The coming of Christ here described is not his second coming to the earth. He comes to the Ancient of days in Heaven to receive dominion, and glory, and a kingdom, which will be given him at the close of his work as a mediator. It is this coming, and not his second advent to the earth, that was foretold in prophecy to take place at the termination of the 2300 days, in 1844. Attended by heavenly angels, our great High Priest enters the holy of holies, and there appears in the presence of God, to engage in the last acts of his ministration in behalf of man,—to perform the work of investigative Judgment, and to make an atonement for all who are shown to be entitled to its benefits. *1888 GC 479-480*

The Clear and Present Paraphrase

11. I continued watching as the vision transitioned to the close of the judgment, and I could hear the Little Horn blaspheming God with his words. I then witnessed the Beast that was controlled by the Little Horn being destroyed and his body being burned in hellfire. The Beast's destruction revealed the punishment given to those who followed the system set up by Rome.

12. By this time, Egypt, Assyria, Babylon, Medo-Persia, and Greece's period of dominance will have already passed, but their influence of false worship and hostility towards God's people will continue to live through Rome until God decides its season of dominance is finished.

13. I then saw another vision that night. It was as if God took me back to the start of the judgment that begins in heaven. Jesus, the One who is often called The Son of Man, was surrounded by so many angels that He looked as if He was riding on a cloud. These angels brought the Son of God to the Most Holy Place within the heavenly sanctuary before The Father, The One who precedes time.

KJV Bible	Daniel Commentary
14. And there was given him dominion, and glory, and a kingdom, that all people, nations, and languages, should serve him: his dominion *is* an everlasting dominion, which shall not pass away, and his kingdom *that* which shall not be destroyed. 15. I Daniel was grieved in my spirit in the midst of *my* body, and the visions of my head troubled me. 16. I came near unto one of them that stood by, and asked him the truth of all this. So he told me, and made me know the interpretation of the things.	14. **Given him dominion** - In Luke 19:12-15, Christ is represented as a nobleman who took his journey into a far country to receive for himself a kingdom and to return. At the close of his priestly ministry in the sanctuary while still in heaven, Christ receives the kingdom from His Father and then returns to the earth for His saints (SDA Bible Commentary Vol 4 pg. 830) 15. **Grieved** - "to be distressed." 16. **One of them** - Daniel is still in vision and is likely being addressed by one of the heavenly attendants at the judgment.

EG White Notes

In the service of the earthly sanctuary, which, as we have seen, is a figure of the service in the heavenly, when the high priest on the day of atonement entered the most holy place, the ministration in the first apartment ceased. God commanded, "There shall be no man in the tabernacle of the congregation when he goeth in to make an atonement in the holy place, until he come out." [Leviticus 16:17.] So when Christ entered the holy of holies to perform the closing work of the atonement, he ceased his ministration in the first apartment. But when the ministration in the first apartment ended, the ministration in the second apartment began. When in the typical service the high priest left the holy on the day of atonement, he went in before God to present the blood of the sin-offering in behalf of all Israel who truly repented of their sins. So Christ had only completed one part of his work as our intercessor, to enter upon another portion of the work, and he still pleaded his blood before the Father in behalf of sinners. *1888 GC 428*

The Clear and Present Paraphrase

14. I then saw that once the judgment was finished, God would take back this world from Satan and give it to the rightful heir—His Son. He will be made ruler over all nations and every language so that people everywhere should serve Him. His authority will be an everlasting authority, and His sovereignty will never end.

15. Now once the vision ended, I was really bothered by what I had seen. I was troubled because I wasn't completely sure what God was trying to tell me.

16. Then I looked up and realized I was still in vision. I know this because I was still seeing the throne of God. So I decided to approach one of the angels present there, and I asked him what all of this meant. And this is what he told me:

KJV Bible	Daniel Commentary
17. These great beasts, which are four, *are* four kings, *which* shall arise out of the earth.	17. **Four kings** - See vs. 3-6. Kings and Kingdoms are often used interchangeably (see vs. 23).
18. But the saints of the most High shall take the kingdom, and possess the kingdom for ever, even for ever and ever.	18. **Take the kingdom** – In the original language, this can mean to take or receive. The rule of the wicked may last for a time, but soon it will come to an end, and this earth will be restored to its rightful Owner. **For ever, even for ever and ever** - The repetition of the phrase emphasizes the idea of eternity.
19. Then I would know the truth of the fourth beast, which was diverse from all the others, exceeding dreadful, whose teeth *were of* iron, and his nails *of* brass; which devoured, brake in pieces, and stamped the residue with his feet;	19. **Know the truth** - Compare vs. 7. Daniel repeats the specifications earlier described. He is interested in the fourth beast, which was unusual in its appearance and its activity when compared to the beasts that preceded it.

EG White Notes

During the thousand years between the first and the second resurrection the judgment of the wicked takes place. The apostle Paul points to this judgment as an event that follows the second advent. "Judge nothing before the time, until the Lord come, who both will bring to light the hidden things of darkness, and will make manifest the counsels of the hearts." 1 Corinthians 4:5. Daniel declares that when the Ancient of Days came, "judgment was given to the saints of the Most High." Daniel 7:22. At this time the righteous reign as kings and priests unto God. John in the Revelation says: "I saw thrones, and they sat upon them, and judgment was given unto them." "They shall be priests of God and of Christ, and shall reign with Him…" Revelation 20:4, 6. It is at this time that, as foretold by Paul, "the saints shall judge the world." 1 Corinthians 6:2. In union with Christ they judge the wicked, comparing their acts with the statute book, the Bible, and deciding every case according to the deeds done in the body. Then the portion which the wicked must suffer is meted out, according to their works; and it is recorded against their names in the book of death. *GC 660-661*

The Clear and Present Paraphrase

17. "These are the four great world powers that will successively dominate the earth from your time until the end of the world.

18. However, those who give their hearts to the Lord will inherit the earth and become citizens of God's kingdom. This is the kingdom that will ultimately supersede all these other kingdoms and will last forever."

19. I listened, but I just had to know more about this Roman Empire. The fact that its kingship will switch from kings to Popes made this power different from all the other powers. Also, knowing this kingdom will dominate the world by crushing every nation in its path really got my attention.

20. And of the ten horns that *were* in his head, and *of* the other which came up, and before whom three fell; even *of* that horn that had eyes, and a mouth that spake very great things, whose look *was* more stout than his fellows.

21. I beheld, and the same horn made war with the saints, and prevailed against them;

22. Until the Ancient of days came, and judgment was given to the saints of the most High; and the time came that the saints possessed the kingdom.

20. **Stout** – Meaning in the original language: "captain," "chief," "great," "lord," or "master." Though initially small and insignificant, this Little Horn grew until it became great. The Roman kingship would eventually become greater than the previous kingships in power and might.

21. **Made war with the saints** – Transitioning to the second phase of Rome, this Little Horn here represents the Papacy's attempt to exterminate the people of God. **Prevailed against them** - For more than a thousand years, the saints seemed helpless against this destructive force.

22. **Ancient of days came** – (See vs. 9) God, the Father, arrives onto the prophetic scene. **Judgment was given** - Judgment would not only be given in favor of the saints, but the saints will one day assist in the work of judgment during the 1000 years. (See 1Cor 6:2-3)

EG White Notes

Little by little, at first in stealth and silence, and then more openly as it increased in strength and gained control of the minds of men, "the mystery of iniquity" carried forward its deceptive and blasphemous work. Almost imperceptibly the customs of heathenism found their way into the Christian church. *1888 GC 49*

The Clear and Present Paraphrase

20. I wanted to know more about those ten kingships whose territories were absorbed into the Roman Empire. Likewise, I was curious to understand more about the three kingships that were destroyed by this empire. I also wanted to know how this nation continued to seek more power and how its Popes blasphemed against God. And last but not least, I really wanted to understand how this nation began so small and insignificant but quickly became so great and powerful.

21. Then, I saw that this same religious power, led by Popes and priests, will persecute the true believers of God, and no one will stand in its way!

22. It was then revealed to me that this war against the saints will continue until God the Father announces judgment in favor of His people and the time arrives for them to have dominion over the earth. I now realized why this judgment scene was so important!

23. Thus he said, The fourth beast shall be the fourth kingdom upon earth, which shall be diverse from all kingdoms, and shall devour the whole earth, and shall tread it down, and break it in pieces.

24. And the ten horns out of this kingdom *are* ten kings *that* shall arise: and another shall rise after them; and he shall be diverse from the first, and he shall subdue three kings.

23. **Devour** – To eat, consume.
24. **Ten kings** – The ten horns represent the ten kingships that ruled prior to Rome's dominance:
    1. Egyptian Kings
    2. Assyrian Kings
    3. Babylonian Kings
    4. Median Kings
    5. Persian Kings
    6. Greek King
    7. Asia-Minor Kings (north)
    8. Ptolemaic Kings (south)
    9. Seleucid Kings (east)
    10. Macedonian Kings (west)

From the first - Better translated, "from the former [horns]." The word for "first" is plural. **Diverse from the first** – The Little Horn was unique because it transitioned from a political power to a religious kingdom. **Three kings** - There were ultimately four kings who controlled Greece following Alexander the Great's death. However, in 281 BC, Seleucus conquered the territory of Asia Minor in the north, leaving three remaining kingships: Macedonia in the west, Seleucia in the east, and Ptolemaic Egypt in the south. These three remaining territories from Greece were the three horns subdued by Rome.

Daniel 7

EG White Notes — The Clear and Present Paraphrase

The symbols of earthly governments are wild beasts. *The Watchman December 24, 1907*

23. Then the angel provided more details about Rome. He said to me, "As you've seen, the Kingdom of Rome will be the fourth kingdom in a series of world-ruling empires. You also saw how Rome will crush all other nations in order to dominate the world.

24. The ten horns that you saw represent the kings of Egypt, Assyria, Babylon, Media, Persia, Greece, and the four kingdoms that will rule the divided Greek Empire. If you remember, those four Greek kingdoms were north, south, east, and west. Prior to Rome's dominance, Eastern Greece, which will be ruled by Seleucus, will conquer Northern Greece, which will be ruled by Lysimachus. This conflict will leave the divided Greek Empire with three horns instead of four. As Rome begins conquering the known world, it will subdue the remaining three kingships of the divided Greek Empire—the Macedonian Kings in the west, the Seleucid Kings in the east, and the Ptolemaic Kings in the south.

25. And he shall speak *great* words against the most High, and shall wear out the saints of the most High, and think to change times and laws: and they shall be given into his hand until a time and times and the dividing of time.

25. Great words - Simply, "words." "Great" is supplied. **Wear out** - Persecution. **Times** - A term meaning a fixed time, as in Daniel 3:7, or meaning a period of time as in Daniel 2:16. The Little Horn endeavored to change the time of the Lord's Sabbath as an attempt to exercise its authority in place of God. **Laws** – This is evidently God's law seeing that civil laws are often changed by those in authority, and such changes would never become the subject of a prophetic vision. **A time and times and the dividing of time** - Here's how this phrase is calculated:

Time = One year or 360 days.
Times = Two Years or 720 days.
Dividing or Half of time = Half a year or 180 days.

This time frame equals 1260 days. Using the "day-for-a-year" principle (see Numbers 14:34), we recognize this time period was actually 1260 *years*. This prophetic period began in 538 AD after the Bishop of Rome was given authority by Emperor Justinian. Exactly 1260 years later, the Papacy was overthrown by France in 1798 AD and has never wielded the same power since that time.

EG White Notes

Satan tampered with the fourth commandment also, and essayed to set aside the ancient Sabbath, the day which God had blessed and sanctified, [Genesis 2:2, 3.] and in its stead to exalt the festival observed by the heathen as "the venerable day of the sun." This change was not at first attempted openly. In the first centuries the true Sabbath had been kept by all Christians. They were jealous for the honor of God, and, believing that his law is immutable, they zealously guarded the sacredness of its precepts. But with great subtlety, Satan worked through his agents to bring about his object. That the attention of the people might be called to the Sunday, it was made a festival in honor of the resurrection of Christ. Religious services were held upon it; yet it was regarded as a day of recreation, the Sabbath being still sacredly observed. *1888 GC 52*

..."time and times and the dividing of time," three years and a half, or 1260 days, of Daniel 7. The time during which the papal power was to oppress God's people. This period, as stated in preceding chapters, began with the supremacy of the papacy, A.D. 538, and terminated in 1798. *GC 439*

The Clear and Present Paraphrase

25. However, Rome won't stop there. Soon afterward, the Roman kingship will be overtaken by its religious leaders, known as Popes. As the continuation of the Roman kingship, these Popes will elevate themselves by making declarations and decrees and taking the prerogatives of God. Ultimately, they will be recognized in place of God. The Church that rules over this kingdom will also chain up Bibles, limit the common people from studying the sacred text, and encourage its priests to interpret scriptures for its citizens. And whoever disobeys this religious power's commands will end up being persecuted relentlessly. If that's not enough, the Papacy will also make everyone believe that the Ten Commandments have been changed. They will elevate the first day of the week as the replacement for the seventh-day Sabbath, resulting in most of the Christian world believing the Sabbath has been abolished. However, some will refuse to follow the Papacy, and they will be persecuted by Rome for 1260 years, which will begin in 538 AD and end in 1798 AD.

26. But the judgment shall sit, and they shall take away his dominion, to consume and to destroy *it* unto the end.

27. And the kingdom and dominion, and the greatness of the kingdom under the whole heaven, shall be given to the people of the saints of the most High, whose kingdom *is* an everlasting kingdom, and all dominions shall serve and obey him.

28. Hitherto *is* the end of the matter. As for me Daniel, my cogitations much troubled me, and my countenance changed in me: but I kept the matter in my heart.

26. **The judgment shall sit** - The judgment will soon pass a sentence of extinction upon the Papal power. However, the Scriptures reveal that this power will continue its war against the saints until the very end.

27. **Shall be given** - Here is a reassuring glance at the conclusion of the turmoil and persecution through which the saints have passed. **All dominions** - There will be no friction or disaffection in the earth made new. There will be complete harmony throughout the entire universe.

28. **My cogitations** - "My thoughts." **Troubled me** - "Frightened." **Countenance** - The revelation of the saint's future seemed to overwhelm and sadden the prophet.

EG White Notes

The Lord's purposes for His people have ever been the same. He desires to bestow on the children of men the riches of an eternal inheritance. His kingdom is an everlasting kingdom. When those who choose to become obedient subjects of the Most High are finally saved in the kingdom of glory, God's purpose for mankind will have been fulfilled. *RH, December 26, 1907*

The kingdoms of this world will become the kingdoms of our Lord and of His Christ. The heavenly gates are again to be lifted up, and with ten thousand times ten thousand and thousands of thousands of holy ones, our Saviour will come forth as King of kings and Lord of lords. Jehovah Immanuel shall be King over all the earth; in that day there shall be one Lord, and His name shall be one. "The tabernacle of God is with men, and He will dwell with them, and they shall be His people, and God Himself shall be with them, and be their God." *ST October 28, 1903*

The Clear and Present Paraphrase

26. But the Heavenly Courts will convene and come to a ruling that the Papacy's authority must be eliminated and its worldwide kingdom destroyed.

27. Then God's people will inherit the everlasting kingdom on the earth made new. They will be able to witness the fullness of its majesty, knowing it will last forever. It will also be governed by the Most High God, and everyone there will obey and serve Him from a loving heart."

28. After the angel's words, I came out of the vision, but to be honest with you, I was deeply troubled by what I had witnessed. So troubled that it began to affect my features, and I became pale like a dead man. However, I decided not to tell anyone what I had seen, so I kept it all to myself.

DANIEL 7 - TEST YOUR KNOWLEDGE

1. What do the four winds of Daniel's vision represent? (*p. 141*) _____

2. List the four beasts and the nations they represent. (*p. 142-146*) _____

   _____

   _____

   _____

3. What do the three ribs in the bear's mouth represent? (*p. 142*) _____

   _____

4. What was the meaning of the Bear being raised on one side? (*p. 142*) _____

   _____

5. Who do the ten horns represent? (*p. 160*) _____

   _____

6. Who is the Little Horn? (*p. 148*) _____

7. Who is the Ancient of Days? (*p. 150*) _____

8. Who were the three horns destroyed by the Little Horn? (*p. 160*) _____

   _____

   _____

9. Explain how the Little Horn impacted the seventh-day Sabbath. (*pp. 162-163*)

   _____

10. Explain the meaning of a time, times, and the dividing of time. (*p. 162*) _____

    _____

    _____

Questions for Discussion:

1. What do you think the role of the ten horns might be in the last days?

2. Why do think most Christians reject the idea of the judgment beginning in heaven?

3. Why do you think many people are nervous about God's Judgment?

4. Are you prepared for the Judgment?

God reveals to Daniel a 2300-day prophecy that culminates with the start of the judgment in heaven.

Daniel 8

The Cleansing of the Sanctuary

CHAPTER 8

1. In the third year of the reign of king Belshazzar a vision appeared unto me, *even unto* me Daniel, after that which appeared unto me at the first.
2. And I saw in a vision; and it came to pass, when I saw, that I *was* at Shushan *in* the palace, which *is* in the province of Elam; and I saw in a vision, and I was by the river of Ulai.
3. Then I lifted up mine eyes, and saw, and, behold, there stood before the river a ram which had *two* horns: and the *two* horns *were* high; but one *was* higher than the other, and the higher came up last.
4. I saw the ram pushing westward, and northward, and southward; so that no beasts might stand before him, neither *was there any* that could deliver out of his hand; but he did according to his will, and became great.

CHAPTER 8

1. **At the first** - Most likely a reference to the vision of chapter 7.
2. **Ulai** - An unidentified river. Some scholars see it as a canal between the Choaspes and the Coprates rivers.
3. **A ram which had two horns** - This beast is later identified as the symbol representing the kings of Media and Persia (vs. 20). **Higher than the other** - Although it rose after Media, Persia became the dominant power when Cyrus defeated Astyages of Media in 553 or 550. The Medes, however, were not treated as inferiors or as a conquered people, but rather as allies.
4. **Pushing westward** – Persia's king pushed westward into Babylon, northward into Assyria, and southward into Egypt. So successful were Persian arms that in the days of Ahasuerus (Esther 1:1), the empire extended from India to Ethiopia, the eastern and southern extremities of the then-known world. **Became great** - Literally, "did great things," or "made himself big," or "magnified himself."

CHAPTER 8

Honored by men with the responsibilities of state and with the secrets of kingdoms bearing universal sway, Daniel was honored by God as His ambassador, and was given many revelations of the mysteries of ages to come. *PK 547*

From the rise and fall of nations as made plain in the books of Daniel and the Revelation, we need to learn how worthless is mere outward and worldly glory. Babylon, with all its power and magnificence, the like of which our world has never since beheld,—power and magnificence which to the people of that day seemed so stable and enduring,—how completely has it passed away! As "the flower of the grass," it has perished. James 1:10. So perished the Medo-Persian kingdom, and the kingdoms of Grecia and Rome. And so perishes all that has not God for its foundation. Only that which is bound up with His purpose, and expresses His character, can endure. His principles are the only steadfast things our world knows. *PK 548*

CHAPTER 8

1. A couple of years later, I had another vision. This vision seemed to be related to the previous one, but I was given a little more detail this time.

2. This particular vision was given to me while I was on official business for the king at his other palace in Susa, which is in the province of Elam. It happened as I was taking a walk along the Ulai River.

3. In this vision, I saw a river. Standing next to that river was a ram with two horns representing the kings who co-ruled this nation. I realized one kingdom would have power over the other when I saw one of its horns was higher than the other, even though it arose last.

4. This nation, symbolized as a ram, will conquer westward, in the direction of Babylon, northward, in the direction of Assyria, and southward, in the direction of Egypt. No other nation will be able to withstand this kingdom or defend against it. This nation will do whatever it wants, and as a result, it will become powerful.

5. And as I was considering, behold, an he goat came from the west on the face of the whole earth, and touched not the ground: and the goat *had* a notable horn between his eyes.

6. And he came to the ram that had *two* horns, which I had seen standing before the river, and ran unto him in the fury of his power.

7. And I saw him come close unto the ram, and he was moved with choler against him, and smote the ram, and brake his two horns: and there was no power in the ram to stand before him, but he cast him down to the ground, and stamped upon him: and there was none that could deliver the ram out of his hand.

8. Therefore the he goat waxed very great: and when he was strong, the great horn was broken; and for it came up four notable ones toward the four winds of heaven.

5. **Goat** – Identified by the angel as representing Greece (vs. 21), also known as the Macedonian Empire of Alexander the Great. **From the west** – Greece lay west of the Persian Empire. **Touched not the ground** – A description fitting for the king that conquered the world so quickly. **Notable horn** – According to vs. 21, this notable horn represents the first great Grecian king, Alexander the Great.

7. **Smote the ram** – We are now shown how absolute Alexander's domination of Persia was.

8. **When he was strong, the great horn was broken** - Here, prophecy accurately predicted that Alexander would fall while his empire was at the height of its power. At the age of 32, still in the prime of life, Alexander died. **Four notable ones** - On the four notable Macedonian (or Hellenistic) kingdoms into which Alexander's empire was divided (See chapter 7:6; 11:3-4).

EG White Notes

Alexander and Caesar found it much easier to subdue a kingdom than to rule their own spirits. After conquering nations, the world's so-called great men fell, one of them through the indulgence of appetite, a victim of intemperance, the other through presumption and mad ambition. *4T 348*

The Clear and Present Paraphrase

5. Now, while I was trying to process what I had just witnessed, a creature resembling a goat suddenly came upon the scene. This animal represented a nation that would rise to prominence in the west. This nation will conquer the known world faster than all its predecessors, which is why the goat never touched the ground in the vision. One other thing I noticed about the goat is he had a large horn between his eyes.

6. I continued watching this goat moving towards the ram. Then as the goat got closer, it charged at the ram with a full head of steam.

7. I watched as the goat violently slammed into the ram, destroying him and both of his horns. The nation represented by the Ram was destroyed by the nation symbolized by the goat, and no other nation helped the ram.

8. The ruler of this nation is symbolized by the goat's large horn, which will continue to grow in strength and power. However, at the height of his power, he will be broken, and in his place, four lesser kings will begin consolidating territory towards the north, south, east, and west.

9. And out of one of them came forth a little horn, which waxed exceeding great, toward the south, and toward the east, and toward the pleasant *land*.

10. And it waxed great, *even* to the host of heaven; and it cast down *some* of the host and of the stars to the ground, and stamped upon them.

9. **Out of one of them** - The word "them" refers to the four winds of heaven. In other words, from out of one of the four points of the compass, another power would rise. **A little horn** - This horn represents the kings of Rome in its Pagan form and the Popes of Rome in its Papal form. **The south, and toward the east** – Rome came from the west and conquered the Seleucid kings in the east and the Ptolemaic kings of the Egyptian south. **Pleasant** - *Tsebiy*, generally means "prominence" or "glorious." The word "Land" was supplied by the translators and is not part of the original text; therefore, we can conclude this verse is not referring to Jerusalem. "The pleasant" points to the prominence that only God can demand. Thus, we see a shift from the little horn symbolizing Pagan kings to representing Catholic Popes

10. **Host of heaven** - Under the new covenant, believers enter the heavenly sanctuary by faith. (See Hebrews 10:19). Therefore, new covenant believers, spiritually, become the company of heaven or what Daniel calls "*the host of heaven.*"

EG White Notes

And he opened his mouth in blasphemy against God, to blaspheme His holy name, and His tabernacle, and them that dwell in heaven. ... And all that dwell upon the earth shall worship Him, whose names are not written in the book of life of the Lamb slain from the foundation of the world." [Revelation 13:6, 8.]

There will be but two classes on the world, those who worship God and keep His commandments, and those who worship the beast and his image. These two classes are in decided opposition to one another. The worshippers of the beast will persecute those who keep the commandments of God. The members of the Roman Catholic church and of the Protestant churches will unite against the remnant people of God. *Ms 18, 1904*

So long has the papacy taken power to itself and ruled over kings and emperors, that the pope aspires to go still further, and make his throne as the throne of God. This is why he is called in prophecy "the man of sin, who opposeth and exalteth himself above all that is called God, or that is worshipped." [2 Thessalonians 2:3, 4.] *Ms 115, 1894*

The Clear and Present Paraphrase

9. The kings of these four kingdoms will fight against each other until another nation rises in the west. Symbolized by a little horn, the kings who consecutively rule this nation will begin as a small insignificant kingship but will ultimately become the most powerful kings in the world. In their quest for world dominion, the kings who rule this nation will conquer the remaining territories of the east and the south. Centuries after these kings conquer the known world, they will attempt to conquer a new frontier—the glorious things of God.

10. As Church and State combine, these kings will become more religio-political. They will also become exceedingly powerful—especially against God's people, who will be considered as bright lights in the Kingdom of Heaven. Through deception, the little horn will not only cause the downfall of God's people, but this power will also annihilate them.

11. Yea, he magnified *himself* even to the prince of the host, and by him the daily *sacrifice* was taken away, and the place of his sanctuary was cast down.

11. Prince of the host - Christ. **Daily sacrifice** - "Sacrifice" is a supplied word that was erroneously added by the translators, so our focus will be on "The Daily." In Hebrew, *tamid* (daily) means "regular," "continual," or "continually." Once we understand that those who accept Christ become spiritual Israel, the definition of the Daily becomes clear. The Bible says - "*...And if ye be Christ's, then are ye Abraham's seed...*" Gal 3:28-29. The Bible also says, "*But he is a Jew, which is one inwardly...*" Rom 2:29. Therefore, we can conclude that Christianity hasn't replaced Israel, but rather Christianity is a CONTINUATION of Israel. What Daniel, on multiple occasions, calls the *daily* or the *continual* is how he identified spiritual Israel, which is also known as the New Testament Church. **Place** – According to Eph 2:6, believers are spiritually in "*heavenly places*." Knowing that Gentiles trodded the temple and the Holy City in heavenly places (Rev 11:1-2) reveals that the little horn's prohibition of Christianity, spiritually, was the casting down of the place of Christ's sanctuary.

Then I saw in relation to the "Daily," that the word "sacrifice" was supplied by man's wisdom, and does not belong to the text; and that the Lord gave the correct view of it to those who gave the judgment hour cry. *Present Truth November 1, 1850*

When union existed, before 1844, nearly all were united on the correct view of the "daily"; but in the confusion since 1844, other views have been embraced, and darkness and confusion have followed. Time has not been a test since 1844, and it will never again be a test. *EW 75*

11. But the little horn won't stop there. These kings will then begin elevating themselves in an attempt to take the place of Christ, the Prince of heaven's people. These religious kings will do everything in their power to take away the continuation of Judaism called Christianity, and through deception and persecution, will employ measures designed to block God's people from their connection to God's heavenly sanctuary.

12. And an host was given *him* against the daily *sacrifice* by reason of transgression, and it cast down the truth to the ground; and it practised, and prospered.

13. Then I heard one saint speaking, and another saint said unto that certain *saint* which spake, How long *shall be* the vision *concerning* the daily *sacrifice*, and the transgression of desolation, to give both the sanctuary and the host to be trodden under foot?

12. **Host** - This appears to be a host of earthly people. Most likely, the nations used by the Papacy to further its agenda. **Cast down the truth** - The Papacy substituted the truth with its own traditions and superstitions (i.e., Sunday Sabbath, purgatory, confession...etc.).

13. **How long?** - The question in the Hebrews literally says - "*How long the vision, the continual, the desolating transgression to give both the sanctuary and the host to trampling.*" **Transgression of desolation** - The transgression and abomination of desolation are the same. Whenever Satanic components are mixed with Godly components, this is called an abomination. The first abomination occurred when Rome's soldiers brought their Pagan superstitions on the grounds of God's holy city. This abomination resulted in the desolation of Jerusalem in 70 AD. In Daniel 8, the transgression of desolation represents the mixing of Paganism and Christianity that became known as Roman Catholicism. In 538 AD, this mixture was established, and God's people were desolated for 1260 years.

EG White Notes

What God intended to do for the world through Israel, the chosen nation, He will finally accomplish through His church. He has entrusted "His vineyard to other vinedressers," who faithfully "render to Him the fruits in their seasons." These witnesses for God are the spiritual Israel, and God will fulfill to them all the covenant promises He made to His ancient people. *Royalty and Ruin 250*

The Clear and Present Paraphrase

12. A vast amount of people within the Roman Empire will become believers in this false system of religion and will persecute those who are part of the continuation of Judaism called Christianity. All of this will happen because everyone will be deceived into breaking the law of God. As the centuries pass, the truth will be more suppressed and dragged down to the point that most of the world will believe the religion of these kings is the true universal religion of God.

13. While still in vision, I then heard two angels talking. One of them said to the other, "How long is the vision regarding the continuation of Judaism called Christianity, and the Pagan-Christian mixture known as Catholicism that brings ruin, and the assault against the heavenly sanctuary and the host of believers that enter it by faith?"

KJV Bible	Daniel Commentary
14. And he said unto me, Unto two thousand and three hundred days; then shall the sanctuary be cleansed.	14. **Unto me** - Some translations read, "unto him." **Days** - Literally, "evening morning." In chapter 8, no date is indicated for the start of the 2300 days. The only place we find a starting period is chapter 9:25. Utilizing the day-for-a-year principle (Ezekiel 4:6), the time is understood to have begun in the year 457 BC, reaching to autumn of 1844 AD (See further comment in Chapter 9). **Sanctuary** - 2300 years takes us past the era of the earthly sanctuary; therefore, the temple cannot refer to the temple in Jerusalem, which was destroyed in 70 AD. The sanctuary of the new covenant is clearly the sanctuary in heaven. (Hebrews 8:1-2) **Be cleansed** - "to be just." The earthly sanctuary consisted of two main divisions, the daily and the yearly. The yearly service was called the Day of Atonement. This was one day out of the year that the sanctuary was freed or cleansed from the sins of the people (see Leviticus 16). This annual cleansing of the sanctuary was a shadow of the real work to be done in the heavenly sanctuary.

EG White Notes

At the termination of the 2300 days, in 1844, no sanctuary had existed on earth for many centuries; therefore the sanctuary in heaven must be the one brought to view in the declaration, "Unto two thousand and three hundred days; then shall the sanctuary be cleansed." But how could the sanctuary in heaven need cleansing? Turning again to the Scriptures, the students of prophecy learned that the cleansing was not a removal of physical impurities, for it was to be accomplished with blood, and therefore must be a cleansing from sin. Thus says the apostle: "It was therefore necessary that the patterns of things in the heavens should be purified with these [the blood of animals]; but the heavenly things themselves with better sacrifices than these [even the precious blood of Christ]." Hebrews 9:23. *4SP 262*

After His ascension, our Saviour was to begin His work as our High Priest. As Christ's ministration was to consist of two great divisions, each occupying a period of time and having a distinctive place in the heavenly sanctuary, so the typical ministration consisted of two divisions, the daily and the yearly service. *CCH 347*

The Clear and Present Paraphrase

14. Then that other angel turned to me as if I had asked the question and said, "After 2300 years, God will do what the Jewish High Priest does in the earthly sanctuary on The Day of Atonement—He will go into the Most Holy place in the heavenly sanctuary and purify it. This is where God opens the books of heaven, and the work of judgment begins. God will vindicate His Name and His people."

15. And it came to pass, when I, *even I* Daniel, had seen the vision, and sought for the meaning, then, behold, there stood before me as the appearance of a man.
16. And I heard a man's voice between *the banks of* Ulai, which called, and said, Gabriel make this *man* to understand the vision.
17. So he came near where I stood: and when he came, I was afraid, and fell upon my face: but he said unto me, Understand, O son of man: for at the time of the end *shall be* the vision.

15. **Sought for the meaning** - Daniel did not understand what he had seen. This is not an uncommon situation as there are times the bearers of a prophetic message need to study the message themselves in order to discover its meaning (1 Peter 1:10-12).
16. **Between the banks** – The voice Daniel heard coming from the Ulai River was the voice of Christ, who appeared to be hovering upon the water (see also Daniel 12:6). **Gabriel** - The same angelic being that announced the birth of John the Baptist (Luke 1:11-20).
17. **Time of the end** - The vision reached until the time when the desolating power known as the Papacy would be destroyed. This event would coincide with the second coming of Christ (2 Thessalonians 2:8).

EG White Notes

As Christ at His ascension appeared in the presence of God to plead sinner's behalf. The blood of Christ, while it was to release the repentant sinner from the condemnation of the law, was not to cancel the sin; it would stand on record in the sanctuary until the final atonement; so in the type the blood of the sin offering removed the sin from the penitent, but it rested in the sanctuary until the day of atonement. In the great day of final award, the dead are to be "judged out of those things which were written in the books, according to their works." Revelation 20:12. Then by virtue of the atoning blood of Christ, the sins of all the truly penitent will be blotted from the books of heaven. Thus the sanctuary will be freed, or cleansed, from the record of sin. In the type, this great work of atonement, or blotting out of sins, was represented by the services of the Day of Atonement—the cleansing of the earthly sanctuary, which was accomplished by the removal, by virtue of the blood of the sin offering, of the sins by which it had been polluted. *CCH 347-348*

The Clear and Present Paraphrase

15. So that's what I saw in the vision, but I still didn't understand it. I tried to make sense of what I had just seen and what the angel told me, but I was still confused about what it all meant. Then, suddenly, another angel appeared in front of me; this one had human features about him.

16. Then I heard a voice say, "Gabriel, explain the vision to Daniel and help him understand it."

17. Then Gabriel came towards me. What a sight! His countenance beamed with the pure light of heaven. As he got closer, I could sense the awesome and glorious power of God Almighty, and I could tell that he came directly from the presence of God Himself! In fact, I was so overwhelmed with awe and reverence that it got to the point that my body began to tremble, and it felt like at any moment, I would be snuffed out of existence! At that point, all I could do was fall on my face. I then heard Gabriel talking to me. "Daniel," he began, "though you may not understand everything you've seen, what you must understand is that the vision extends all the way to the time of the end of the world."

183

18. Now as he was speaking with me, I was in a deep sleep on my face toward the ground: but he touched me, and set me upright.

19. And he said, Behold, I will make thee know what shall be in the last end of the indignation: for at the time appointed the end *shall be*.

20. The ram which thou sawest having *two* horns *are* the kings of Media and Persia.

21. And the rough goat *is* the king of Grecia: and the great horn that *is* between his eyes *is* the first king.

18. **Deep sleep** – It is unlikely that this sleep was the same deep sleep that occurs during overnight sleeping. Instead, it appears Daniel was in a state similar to sleep, but his senses were fully functional as if he were awake (see Num 24:4).

19. **End of indignation** – The anger of the nations and their dominance over God's people.

20. **The ram** - See vs. 3 and 4.

21. **Rough** - "Hairy," or "shaggy." **Great horn** - Symbolic of Alexander the Great, the "first king" of the Greco-Macedonian world empire that would replace the Persian Empire.

EG White Notes

The kingdom was then subject to Babylon. When Babylon fell, and Medo-Persia succeeded, it was overturned the first time. When Medo-Persia fell and was succeeded by Greece, it was overturned the second time. When the Greek empire gave way to Rome, it was overturned the third time. *PP 762*

The crown removed from Israel passed successively to the kingdoms of Babylon, Medo-Persia, Greece, and Rome. *True Education 108*

The Clear and Present Paraphrase

18. This whole conversation had taken place while I was still in vision, and even though I was awake, I must've been in some sort of trance. Then, Gabriel put his hand on me, lifted me off the ground, and placed me back up on my feet.

19. He continued and said, "I want to give you a little more detail around the wars, conquests, and persecution that takes place towards the end of time. However, God won't allow it to continue forever, and He has determined when all this ends.

20. As you already know, the ram that you saw with the two horns represents the joint empire of Media-Persia. However, what you don't know is that the two horns on the ram represent all the kings who rule Media and all the kings who rule Persia.

21. And what about the goat with the great horn? You already know the goat represents the kingdom of Greece, but what you haven't been told is that the great horn between his eyes represents Greece's first king, Alexander the Great.

KJV Bible

22. Now that being broken, whereas four stood up for it, four kingdoms shall stand up out of the nation, but not in his power.

23. And in the latter time of their kingdom, when the transgressors are come to the full, a king of fierce countenance, and understanding dark sentences, shall stand up.

Daniel Commentary

22. Four kingdoms – The four Hellenistic kingdoms that devolved out of Alexander's empire. Asia Minor (north), Seleucia (east), Ptolemaic Egypt (south), Macedonia (west).

23. Latter time – After the divisions of Alexander's kingdom had been in existence for some time, the Roman Empire gradually arose and attained supremacy. **A king** – This represents all the kings who ruled Rome; therefore, "king" here symbolizes both phases of the Roman Empire, including Pagan kings and Catholic Popes. **The Transgressors** – The Greek versions read "sins." **Come to the full** – This could be referring to the various nations, or possibly specifically the Jews, filling up the cup of their iniquity. (See Genesis 15:16). **Fierce countenance** – Possibly an allusion to Deuteronomy 28:49-55. **Dark sentences** – Meaning "mysterious statements." Similar to Numbers 12:8 (dark speeches) Judges 14:12 (riddles). Possibly a reference to the unknown language of the up-and-coming Latin-speaking world power. **Stand up** – Come into power or rulership; reign begins.

EG White Notes

By the Spirit of Inspiration, looking far down the ages, Moses pictured the terrible scenes of Israel's final overthrow as a nation, and the destruction of Jerusalem by the armies of Rome: "The Lord shall bring a nation against thee from far, from the end of the earth, as swift as the eagle flieth; a nation whose tongue thou shalt not understand; a nation of fierce countenance, which shall not regard the person of the old, nor show favor to the young." PP 467

The Clear and Present Paraphrase

22. In the prime of his power, Alexander will suddenly die. This untimely death will send his top generals and closest officials into a frenzy as they attempt to obtain power and territory for themselves. Ultimately, this will cause Greece to fragment into four smaller kingdoms. And though these four kingships will rule the same territory as Alexander the Great, they will never be as great as the Greek King.

23. Centuries later, apostasy will become prevalent. And just when it seems it can't get any worse, another power will rise to conquer the world. This nation will be known as the Roman Empire. Its kings will be brutal and ferocious, and they will speak in a language totally unfamiliar to the children of Israel. This is the nation that will rise to rule the known world.

KJV Bible

24. And his power shall be mighty, but not by his own power: and he shall destroy wonderfully, and shall prosper, and practise, and shall destroy the mighty and the holy people.
25. And through his policy also he shall cause craft to prosper in his hand; and he shall magnify *himself* in his heart, and by peace shall destroy many: he shall also stand up against the Prince of princes; but he shall be broken without hand.

Daniel Commentary

24. **Not by his own power** – This could be consistent with the previous statement that says, "an host was given him" (vs. 12). Some see this as a reference to the Papacy's use of secular governments to enforce its religious objectives. Also, this may be alluding to the fact that Satan, the Dragon, was behind Rome's success (Rev 13:2). The Brenton Septuagint Translation removes this negative clause altogether and translates this verse in the following manner: "...and shall destroy mighty men, and the holy people." **wonderfully** - extraordinary destruction.
25. **Craft** – "Deceit." This is an accurate description of the methods used by the Papal phase of this power. **Prince of princes** – The same individual deemed "the prince of the host" in vs. 11. This was none other than Jesus Christ. **Without hand** – No human hand will participate in this destruction. The Lord Himself will ultimately destroy this power (see chapter 2:34). This religious system will continue until it is destroyed by the hand of God at the Second Coming of Christ (see 2 Thessalonians 2:8).

EG White Notes

The accession of the Roman Church to power marked the beginning of the Dark Ages. As her power increased, the darkness deepened. Faith was transferred from Christ, the true foundation, to the pope of Rome. Instead of trusting in the Son of God for forgiveness of sins and for eternal salvation, the people looked to the pope, and to the priests and prelates to whom he delegated authority. They were taught that the pope was their earthly mediator and that none could approach God except through him; and, further, that he stood in the place of God to them and was therefore to be implicitly obeyed. A deviation from his requirements was sufficient cause for the severest punishment to be visited upon the bodies and souls of the offenders. Thus the minds of the people were turned away from God to fallible, erring, and cruel men, nay, more, to the prince of darkness himself, who exercised his power through them. *GC 55*

The Clear and Present Paraphrase

24. The Roman kingship will become mighty and powerful. They will utilize this power to cause extraordinary destruction to those who oppose them. These kings will prosper in doing everything they can to destroy God's mighty and holy Church.

25. Once the Roman Kingship converts from Paganism to Christianity, they will enact policies for the Church. These policies will spread very quickly at the hands of these kings, who will magnify themselves as having heavenly insight in order to blend Pagan lies with Christian truth. Not only will these kings be responsible for destroying many without a sword, but they will also elevate themselves against Jesus Christ! However, never forget that in the end, this power will be destroyed—not by the hand of humans, but by the Hand of God.

26. And the vision of the evening and the morning which was told *is* true: wherefore shut thou up the vision; for it *shall be* for many days.

27. And I Daniel fainted, and was sick *certain* days; afterward I rose up, and did the king's business; and I was astonished at the vision, but none understood *it*.

26. **Evening and the morning** — This is not the same as "morning and evening," which relate to the temple sacrifices. Evening and mornings refer to a day (see Gen 1:5). Most likely, this refers to the time prophecy of vs. 14 (see comments there). The angel does not provide any more detail regarding the 2300-day prophecy but merely emphasizes its truthfulness. **True** — Guaranteed. **Shut thou up** — Compare similar instructions recorded in chapter 12:4 (see comments there). **For many days** — This means the various details of the vision of this chapter and their fulfillment would extend into the distant future.

27. **I Daniel fainted** — Daniel was clearly concerned about the events that had been revealed to him, and the fact that Gabriel informed the prophet that the ultimate end would be many years in the future may have amplified that concern. **None understood it** — Further information was later given (see chapter 9:23).

The great things to take place are before us and we, all who are living, shall see to the end of these judgments which are before us... We can say, concerning... the many places where the judgments of God have been witnessed, that they are a standing warning to the people..., opening to them what Daniel in vision saw would be. "And the vision of the evening and the morning which was told is true: wherefore shut thou up the vision; for it shall be for many days. And I Daniel fainted, and was sick certain days; afterwards I rose up, and did the king's business; and I was astonished at the vision, but none understood it." Daniel 8:26, 27. *Ms 129 1908*

26. The part of the vision you saw regarding the 2,300 hundred years is guaranteed to happen. However, don't stress yourself out by trying to understand everything you saw because this part of the vision is sealed, and it will be several centuries before it will be revealed."

27. Then I came out of the vision. However, I was so overwhelmed by what I had seen, that for days afterward, I felt sick. Then, I finally went back to work carrying on the king's business, but I was still in awe of what I had seen in the vision and desperately wanted to know what it all meant; however, I just couldn't grasp it.

DANIEL 8 - TEST YOUR KNOWLEDGE

1. Who is the Prince of the Host? *(p. 176)* _____

2. What nation did the ram with two horns represent? *(p. 170)* _____

3. Explain why one horn was higher than the other. *(p. 170)* _____
   _____

4. Explain the cleansing of the sanctuary. *(pp. 180-181)* _____
   _____
   _____

5. What nation was represented by the goat? *(p. 172)* _____

6. Explain what happened when the goat's horn was broken. *(p. 172)* _____
   _____

7. Explain how the 2300-day prophecy refers to years and not days. *(p. 180)* ____
   _____

8. What are the two classes of this world? *(p. 175)* _____
   _____

9. Explain the Daily Sacrifice. *(p. 176)* _____
   _____

10. What marked the beginning of the Dark Ages? *(p. 189)* _____
    _____

Questions for Discussion:

1. Why do you think the vision of chapter 8 began with Media-Persia instead of Babylon?

2. Why do you think Daniel become afraid when he saw the angel?

3. There are many Christians who claim the Little Horn was a Syrian king named Antiochus Epiphanes. How do we determine the Little Horn was the Papacy and not this king?

God gives Daniel a very important message that will not only affect his people but will have major implications on the entire world.

Daniel 9

The Seventy-Weeks Prophecy

CHAPTER 9

1. In the first year of Darius the son of Ahasuerus, of the seed of the Medes, which was made king over the realm of the Chaldeans;
2. In the first year of his reign I Daniel understood by books the number of the years, whereof the word of the LORD came to Jeremiah the prophet, that he would accomplish seventy years in the desolations of Jerusalem.
3. And I set my face unto the Lord God, to seek by prayer and supplications, with fasting, and sackcloth, and ashes:
4. And I prayed unto the LORD my God, and made my confession, and said, O Lord, the great and dreadful God, keeping the covenant and mercy to them that love him, and to them that keep his commandments;

CHAPTER 9

1. **Darius** – There is much dispute regarding the identity of the Babylonian ruler. Because of Daniel's abilities and integrity, the Persians did not execute him but established him in high office. **Which was made king** - Cyrus may have been in the process of rebelling against Media and placed his friend and relative, Darius the Mede, on the Babylonian throne to give the appearance that Media was still a co-ruler with Persia. Cyrus was likely the one in power, and Darius was probably a figurehead.
2. **Understood by books** – Even though Daniel was busy, he continued to study God's Word. **Seventy years** - The fulfillment of the Jeremiah 29:10 prophecy was near, which meant the Jew's captivity would soon expire.
3. **To seek by prayer** - Even though the Lord had promised deliverance to His people, Daniel understood the conditional nature of many of God's promises (see Jeremiah 18:7-10).
4. **Dreadful** - awe-inspiring or revered (see Psalms 111:9).

EG White Notes

CHAPTER 9

A promise had been made, "After seventy years ... I will visit you, and perform My good word toward you." Jeremiah 29:10. Though Daniel was himself a prophet, yet he consulted the scriptural record found in the books. He understood by books that seventy years was the time fixed for the continuance of the desolation of Jerusalem. The book was the prophecies of Jeremiah. God had said, "I will visit you and perform My good word toward you." [Verse 10.] Though Daniel himself was a great prophet, well acquainted with the visions of God, yet he was a diligent searcher of the Scriptures. He thought it wise to consult Jeremiah's prophecies. And he prayed to God aloud most earnestly. *Ms 129, 1908*

The Clear and Present Paraphrase

CHAPTER 9

1. Darius, the son of Ahasuerus of the Medes, was made king over the realm of Babylon.
2. In the first year of his reign, the Lord revealed to me through the book of Jeremiah that Jerusalem would be in ruins for seventy years, and that time period was coming to an end soon.
3. Once I understood this, I began pleading with the Lord in prayer. I also began fasting with sackcloth and ashes.
4. I prayed to the Lord my God, and I confessed my sin and the sins of my people. And this is what I said to Him: "Lord, you are great and awesome. You, who keeps the covenant with those who love you and keep your commandments.

5. We have sinned, and have committed iniquity, and have done wickedly, and have rebelled, even by departing from thy precepts and from thy judgments:
6. Neither have we hearkened unto thy servants the prophets, which spake in thy name to our kings, our princes, and our fathers, and to all the people of the land.
7. O Lord, righteousness *belongeth* unto thee, but unto us confusion of faces, as at this day; to the men of Judah, and to the inhabitants of Jerusalem, and unto all Israel, *that are* near, and *that are* far off, through all the countries whither thou hast driven them, because of their trespass that they have trespassed against thee.
8. O Lord, to us *belongeth* confusion of face, to our kings, to our princes, and to our fathers, because we have sinned against thee.

5. **We have sinned** - Compare 1Kings 8:47; Psalms 106:6. Daniel identifies himself with the Children of Israel. **The prophets** - A role of a prophet is to call the attention of the people to their neglect of God's commandments, as well as to give direction in present emergencies, but the guidance provided had been almost totally ignored. The people's sin was not due to ignorance but to their own willful disobedience.
6. **Righteousness** – The prophet distinguishes the righteousness of God from the unrighteousness of Israel.

EG White Notes

Daniel does not proclaim his own fidelity before the Lord. Instead of claiming to be pure and holy, this honored prophet humbly identifies himself with the really sinful of Israel. The wisdom which God had imparted to him was as far superior to the wisdom of the great men of the world as the light of the sun shining in the heavens at noonday is brighter than the feeblest star. Yet ponder the prayer from the lips of this man so highly favored of Heaven. *Prayer 146*

The Clear and Present Paraphrase

5. Father, we have sinned and committed iniquity. Not only have we sinned and committed iniquity, but we have done disgustingly wicked acts and have done everything contrary to your will.
6. We even ignored your prophets that you sent to us to speak to our kings, princes, leaders, and even our whole nation.
7. Oh Father! You are synonymous with righteousness, and we are synonymous with shame. And that goes for all of us, even the people of Judah, Jerusalem, and Israel who you have scattered among throughout the countries because of the sin they committed against you.
8. All of us have sinned. This includes our kings, our princes, and our leaders. We are all guilty because we have sinned against you.

KJV Bible

9. To the Lord our God *belong* mercies and forgivenesses, though we have rebelled against him;
10. Neither have we obeyed the voice of the LORD our God, to walk in his laws, which he set before us by his servants the prophets.
11. Yea, all Israel have transgressed thy law, even by departing, that they might not obey thy voice; therefore the curse is poured upon us, and the oath that *is* written in the law of Moses the servant of God, because we have sinned against him.

Daniel Commentary

9. **Mercies and forgiveness** -Even though Israel had backslidden and was in full rebellion, Daniel remained confident that the Lord, because of His mercy, was ready to forgive all those who should come to Him with a contrite heart.

11. **Is poured** - Moses had prophesied that a curse such as this would fall upon all who were willfully disobedient to God's law (Leviticus 26:14-41; Deuteronomy 28:15-68).

EG White Notes

With deep humiliation, with tears and rending of heart, he pleads for himself and for his people. He lays his soul open before God, confessing his own unworthiness and acknowledging the Lord's greatness and majesty. *Prayer 146*

The Clear and Present Paraphrase

9. And even though we've done all this against you, you are still merciful and forgiving.
10. Lord, we are supposed to be your people, but yet we have disobeyed you and have refused to follow your laws given to us through your prophets.
11. Yes, all of us have broken your law. We have turned our backs on you, so we can't see you, and have covered our ears so we can't hear your voice. And this is why all the curses written by Moses are being poured on us. All of this is happening because we have sinned against you.

12. And he hath confirmed his words, which he spake against us, and against our judges that judged us, by bringing upon us a great evil: for under the whole heaven hath not been done as hath been done upon Jerusalem.

13. As *it is* written in the law of Moses, all this evil is come upon us: yet made we not our prayer before the LORD our God, that we might turn from our iniquities, and understand thy truth.

14. Therefore hath the LORD watched upon the evil, and brought it upon us: for the LORD our God *is* righteous in all his works which he doeth: for we obeyed not his voice.

15. And now, O Lord our God, that hast brought thy people forth out of the land of Egypt with a mighty hand, and hast gotten thee renown, as at this day; we have sinned, we have done wickedly.

16. O Lord, according to all thy righteousness, I beseech thee, let thine anger and thy fury be turned away from thy city Jerusalem, thy holy mountain: because for our sins, and for the iniquities of our fathers, Jerusalem and thy people *are become* a reproach to all *that are* about us.

12. **Our judges** - Used in a wide sense to signify kings, princes, and rulers generally (compare Hosea 7:7).

13. **As it is written** - See Deuteronomy 29:21,27.

14. **Watched** - Meaning, "to be on the alert," "to be wakeful."

15. **Brought thy people forth** - Daniel refers to the former great deliverance of the children of Israel from the Egyptian bondage and bases his request upon the great act of mercy performed by the Lord at the time of the Exodus.

16. **Righteousness** - Daniel's plea is not contingent on the goodness of his people, but rather it is contingent on the Lord's gracious dealings with Israel in times past. **Thy holy mountain** - Israel was supposed to have been a light to all the world (Isaiah 42:6, Acts 13:47). However, they were now being used as an example of a rebuke among the nations of the earth.

EG White Notes

What a prayer was that which came forth from the lips of Daniel! What humbling of soul it reveals! The warmth of heavenly fire was recognized in the words that were going upward to God. *That I May Know Him 271*

The Clear and Present Paraphrase

12. All this has shown us that your Word is true. You warned us of the consequences, yet because of our disobedience, Jerusalem has been ravished more than any other city in the world.

13. Moses told us what would happen, but we didn't care. We kept sinning against you and refused to pray for deliverance from our wicked desires in order to understand your will.

14. Lord, I know you patiently waited. However, I also know you eventually had to discipline us. But Lord, even in punishment, you are righteous.

15. You are the same God who rescued us and brought us out of Egypt. This rescue wasn't a small event, but you did it with a great display of power that made a lasting impression even to this day. But even after all of that, we still find ourselves sinning against you.

16. Father, you've always done what is right. Please don't let Jerusalem continue to be punished for our sins and the unrepentant wickedness of our ancestors. Even the heathens are calling us a disgrace!

17. Now therefore, O our God, hear the prayer of thy servant, and his supplications, and cause thy face to shine upon thy sanctuary that is desolate, for the Lord's sake.

18. O my God, incline thine ear, and hear; open thine eyes, and behold our desolations, and the city which is called by thy name: for we do not present our supplications before thee for our righteousnesses, but for thy great mercies.

19. O Lord, hear; O Lord, forgive; O Lord, hearken and do; defer not, for thine own sake, O my God: for thy city and thy people are called by thy name.

20. And whiles I *was* speaking, and praying, and confessing my sin and the sin of my people Israel, and presenting my supplication before the LORD my God for the holy mountain of my God;

17. **Cause thy face to shine** - Meaning, "look with favor." **Sanctuary** - Daniel's mind was focused on the sanctuary in Jerusalem as it was in ruins; however, the time for rebuilding was near.

19. **Defer** - "to delay," "to hesitate." Daniel was anxious and was hoping that the promised deliverance would no longer be delayed.

EG White Notes

Daniel's heart was burdened for the people of God, for the city and temple that were laid waste. His deepest interest was for the honor of God and the prosperity of Israel. It was this that moved him to seek God with prayer and fasting and deep humiliation. *RH February 9, 1897*

The Clear and Present Paraphrase

17. So we humbly ask that you hear this prayer and that you please look favorably on Jerusalem and your temple. However, not for our sake but, Lord, for your sake.
18. Please hear my prayer, oh Lord. Incline your ear. Don't close your eyes toward me but see how your city is in ruins even now. Father, we know we don't deserve anything, but we also know that you are merciful.
19. Father, please hear me! Please forgive us! Do not delay our deliverance! We believe in your promises. Lord, Jerusalem is your city, and we are your people."
20. Now, right while I was in the middle of praying and confessing my sins and Israel's sins

Daniel 9

KJV Bible

21. Yea, whiles I *was* speaking in prayer, even the man Gabriel, whom I had seen in the vision at the beginning, being caused to fly swiftly, touched me about the time of the evening oblation.
22. And he informed *me*, and talked with me, and said, O Daniel, I am now come forth to give thee skill and understanding.
23. At the beginning of thy supplications the commandment came forth, and I am come to shew *thee*; for thou *art* greatly beloved: therefore understand the matter, and consider the vision.

Daniel Commentary

21. **Gabriel** - This is the same being who had explained the first three sections of the vision of chapter 8. He now returns to Daniel in order to complete his assigned task.
22. **Understanding** – In order to see what Daniel needed to understand, we must acknowledge the close connection between chapters 8 and 9. The 2300 days is the only component of Daniel 8's vision that Gabriel did not fully explain. All the other symbols in Daniel 8:2-14 are explained in verses 15-26 of the same chapter.
23. **Consider the vision** – This is an apparent reference to "the vision of the evening and the morning" (chapter 8:26). As an answer to his prayer, Gabriel, who had been commissioned to explain the vision of chapter 8 but had not yet completed the explanation, greets Daniel by saying, "I am now come forth to give thee skill and understanding." Knowing Daniel's focus was on the captivity of his people, it is likely that Daniel was trying to understand the relation between the 70 years of captivity and the 2300 days for the cleansing of the sanctuary.

EG White Notes

The spirit of intercession was upon Daniel, and he laid hold of the throne of infinite power, praying earnestly for the restoration of Jerusalem. All heaven was interested in his supplication, and before his prayer was finished, a messenger from the heavenly courts was sent to him. *Ms 138, 1899*

There was only one point in the vision of chapter eight which had been left unexplained, namely, that relating to time,—the period of the 2300 days; therefore, the angel, in resuming his explanation, dwells exclusively upon the subject of time. *1888 GC 325*

The Clear and Present Paraphrase

21. Gabriel, the same angel I had seen earlier, showed up again. This was around the time of the evening offering.

22. "Daniel," he said, "I have come back to give you a better understanding and more insight regarding the vision.

23. As soon as you began praying, God gave me a command to help you, so I am here because you are precious to God. Now listen closely to what I am about to say so that you can better understand the vision previously given to you.

24. Seventy weeks are determined upon thy people and upon thy holy city, to finish the transgression, and to make an end of sins, and to make reconciliation for iniquity, and to bring in everlasting righteousness, and to seal up the vision and prophecy, and to anoint the most Holy.

24. Seventy weeks - Applying the day-for-a-year principle (Num 14:34), it is evident that these weeks represent 7-year groups equaling 490 years. **Are determined** - Meaning "to cut," "to cut off." Since chapter 9 is an explanation of the unexplained portion of chapter 8, it is logical to conclude that the 70 weeks or 490 years were taken from the longer 2300-year period and have the same starting point. **To seal up** - To seal up was a means to preserve documents. This is why Isaiah was told to "bind up the testimony, and seal the law" (Isaiah 8:16). With this understanding, Israel was to keep the integrity of the prophecy. **Anoint the most Holy** - "Anoint" in the original language is *"mashac." Mashac* is also translated as consecrate, which is the same action taking place in Isaiah 8:13 - "Sanctify the LORD of hosts..." With this view in mind, the anointing of the Most Holy simply means that the children of Israel had a certain time to regard God as holy and seek to be holy like Him. The time given to the Jewish nation expired in 34 AD and was confirmed by the stoning of Stephen. (Acts 7)

EG White Notes

The time of the first advent and of some of the chief events clustering about the Saviour's lifework was made known by the angel Gabriel to Daniel. "Seventy weeks," said the angel, "are determined upon thy people and upon thy holy city, to finish the transgression, and to make an end of sins, and to make reconciliation for iniquity, and to bring in everlasting righteousness, and to seal up the vision and prophecy, and to anoint the most holy." Daniel 9:24

A day in prophecy stands for a year. See Numbers 14:34; Ezekiel 4:6. The seventy weeks, or four hundred and ninety days, represent four hundred and ninety years. *PK 698*

The seventy weeks, or 490 years, especially allotted to the Jews, ended, as we have seen, in A. D. 34. At that time, through the action of the Jewish Sanhedrim, the nation sealed its rejection of the gospel, by the martyrdom of Stephen and the persecution of the followers of Christ. *1888 GC 328*

The Clear and Present Paraphrase

24. Out of the 2,300 years previously mentioned, you must understand that 490 of those years have been allotted to your people and Jerusalem. Those 490 probationary years are given to your people and Jerusalem in order for them to stop intentionally choosing to disobey God, to turn away from their sins, to be reconciled back to God, to accept God's grace, receive His righteousness which never fades, to preserve the integrity of the vision by living up to its fulfillment, and to sanctify the Lord by recognizing his holiness and authority over them.

KJV Bible	Daniel Commentary
25. Know therefore and understand, *that* from the going forth of the commandment to restore and to build Jerusalem unto the Messiah the Prince *shall be* seven weeks, and threescore and two weeks: the street shall be built again, and the wall, even in troublous times.	**25. Going forth of the commandment** - There were three decrees that could potentially fulfill this prophecy. The first two decrees primarily referred to the restoration of the temple and its worship but did not address the restoration of their civil state. However, the decree that came in the 7th year of Artaxerxes was the only decree that made provision for the restoration of both the religious and the civil government. This decree took place in 457 BC and can be found in Ezra 7:1-26. **Messiah** – "Anointed one." Daniel was shown the long-looked-for Messiah and was shown when Jesus would appear. **Seven weeks and threescore and two weeks** - Seven weeks plus 62 weeks equals 69 weeks. Using the day-for-a-year principle, Jerusalem was rebuilt after the first seven weeks or 49 years in 408 BC. The Messiah's ministry began in 27 AD which was 62 weeks or 434 years after Jerusalem was rebuilt. The decree to rebuild and restore Jerusalem was given in the autumn of 457 BC, and thus Jesus was baptized 69 weeks or 483 years later, in 27 AD.

EG White Notes

A starting point for this period is given: "Know therefore and understand, that from the going forth of the commandment to restore and to build Jerusalem unto the Messiah the Prince shall be seven weeks, and threescore and two weeks" (Daniel 9:25), sixty-nine weeks, or four hundred and eighty-three years.

The commandment to restore and build Jerusalem, as completed by the decree of Artaxerxes Longimanus, went into effect in the autumn of 457 B.C. See Ezra 6:14; 7:1, 9. From this time four hundred and eighty-three years extend to the autumn of A.D. 27. According to the prophecy, this period was to reach to the Messiah, the Anointed One. In A.D. 27, Jesus at His baptism received the anointing of the Holy Spirit and soon afterward began His ministry. Then the message was proclaimed, "The time is fulfilled." Mark 1:15. *PK 698*

The Lord foresaw the troublous times that were to follow during the reign of Xerxes (Ahasuerus of the book of Esther), and He inspired Zechariah to plead with the exiles to return. *FSTS 309*

The Clear and Present Paraphrase

25. Now, it's important that you hear this, but it's also important for you to understand that in the near future, there will be three decrees to restore Jerusalem. The decree that will be of most interest to you and the people of Israel will be the decree that commands the rebuilding of Jerusalem along with the restoration of its religious ministration and civil government. This command, given by King Artaxerxes, will be carried out in 457 BC and is significant because 49 years later, Jerusalem will be completely rebuilt, and 434 years after this restoration, Jesus Christ will emerge as the promised Messiah. By that time, the court in front of the temple will be recreated along with the walls so it will once again be a fortified city. Unfortunately, this restoration will happen during troublesome times as the Persians will attempt to eradicate your people.

KJV Bible

26. And after threescore and two weeks shall Messiah be cut off, but not for himself: and the people of the prince that shall come shall destroy the city and the sanctuary; and the end thereof *shall be* with a flood, and unto the end of the war desolations are determined.

Daniel Commentary

26. After threescore and two weeks – The previous verse focused on the seven weeks (49 years) it took to rebuild Jerusalem) + the 62 weeks (434 years) that remained until Jesus' ministry began. However, this verse bypasses the first seven weeks and solely focuses on the remaining 62 weeks until Jesus' ministry began. Most likely, the first seven weeks, though not mentioned in this verse, are implied with the remaining 62 weeks. **Cut off** - Christ would be crucified sometime after the remaining 62 weeks. **But not for himself** – The sentiment of this phrase is similar to John 14:30, which says, "...the prince of this world cometh, and hath nothing in me." Satan was unable to find any weaknesses in Christ to exploit and ruin the plan of salvation. **And the people** - The Romans. **The city and the sanctuary** - An obliteration of the temple and the city of Jerusalem is here prophesied and was fulfilled in 70 AD by the Romans. **With a flood** - Overwhelming armies of people. **Desolations are determined** - Wars and destruction shall continue until the end.

In the spring of a.d. 31, Christ, the True Sacrifice, was offered on Calvary. Then the veil of the temple was torn in two, showing that the sacrificial service had lost its sacredness and significance. *Humble Hero 100*

Amid national strife and ruin, the steps of the disciples would be beset with perils, and often their hearts would be oppressed by fear. They were to see Jerusalem a desolation, the temple swept away, its worship forever ended, and Israel scattered to all lands, like wrecks on a desert shore. Jesus said, "Ye shall hear of wars and rumors of wars." "Nation shall rise against nation, and kingdom against kingdom: and there shall be famines, and pestilences, and earthquakes, in divers places. All these are the beginning of sorrows." Matthew 24:6-8. Yet Christ's followers were not to fear that their hope was lost or that God had forsaken the earth. *Thoughts From the Mount of Blessing 120*

26. And though the Son of God will emerge 434 years after Jerusalem's restoration, He will be crucified not long afterward. While no fault will be found in the Messiah to warrant this death, those who refuse to accept Him will be slaughtered by the Roman armies, who will also destroy Jerusalem and the sanctuary. Sadly, destruction and war will continue happening until the very end.

27. And he shall confirm the covenant with many for one week: and in the midst of the week he shall cause the sacrifice and the oblation to cease, and for the overspreading of abominations he shall make *it* desolate, even until the consummation, and that determined shall be poured upon the desolate.

27. For one week - The 70th week (which was the last 7-year period) began in 27 AD, which was the opening of Christ's public ministry. **In the midst** - For three and a half years, Christ's ministry was tolerated until He was crucified in 31 AD, which was in the middle of the 70th prophetic week. This also meant that the Jews had $3^{1/2}$ years left to fulfill their part of the vision. However, they continued to reject Christ until their national probation closed in 34 AD. The stoning of Stephen marked the end of the 70th week. Prior to this time, the disciples were commanded to *"Go not into the way of the Gentiles...But go rather to the lost sheep of the house of Israel."* (Matt 10:5-6). However, once Stephen was stoned, the time of national Israel ended, and the time of spiritual Israel began. This is why Paul and Barnabas said, *"It was necessary that the word of God should first have been spoken to you: but seeing ye put it from you, and judge yourselves unworthy of everlasting life, lo, we turn to the Gentiles"* (Acts 13:46). **Cease** - The sacrificial system met its fulfillment and no longer had significance.

EG White Notes

The "week" here brought to view is the last one of the seventy; it is the last seven years of the period allotted especially to the Jews. During this time, extending from A. D. 27 to A. D. 34, Christ, at first in person, and afterward by his disciples, extended the gospel invitation especially to the Jews. As the apostles went forth with the good tidings of the kingdom, the Saviour's direction was, "Go not into the way of the Gentiles, and into any city of the Samaritans enter ye not; but go rather to the lost sheep of the house of Israel. [Matthew 10:5, 6.] "And in the midst of the week he shall cause the sacrifice and the oblation to cease." In A. D. 31, three and a half years after his baptism, our Lord was crucified. With the great sacrifice offered upon Calvary, ended that system of offerings which for four thousand years had pointed forward to the Lamb of God. *1888 GC 327*

The power and the glory belong unto Him whose great purposes would still move on unthwarted toward their consummation. *Thoughts From the Mount of Blessing 120*

The ruin of Jerusalem was a symbol of the final ruin that shall overwhelm the world. *Prayer 303*

The Clear and Present Paraphrase

27. During the last seven of the 490 years allocated to the Jews, Jesus the Messiah will put all His effort into saving the lost sheep of Israel. He will do this by teaching and preaching a new covenant. However, after three and a half years, Jesus will be crucified. His crucifixion will put an end to the earthly sanctuary services and the Levitical laws that point to His death. This will leave Israel with three and a half years remaining until their probation is closed. Unfortunately, your people will continue to reject God's grace and mercy and will continue to do things that God considers an abomination. This will ultimately be the reason behind Jerusalem's destruction by the Roman armies. However, just as surely as Jerusalem will be destroyed, Rome will eventually meet a similar fate."

DANIEL 9 - TEST YOUR KNOWLEDGE

1. How many years were the Jews to be held in captivity? (*pp. 196-197*)_____

2. What book of the Old Testament did Daniel read? (*pp. 196-197*)_____

3. Who showed up while Daniel was praying? (*p. 206*)_____

4. What part of the vision did Daniel need help understanding? (*p. 206*) _____
   _____

5. Using the day for a year principle, how many years is seventy weeks? (*p. 208*)
   _____

6. What happened in the middle of the 70th week? (*p. 214*) _____
   _____

7. Explain what event, Gabriel told Daniel, would indicate the starting point for the seventy-weeks prophecy. (*pp. 210-11*)_____
   _____

8. What even marked the end of the seventy weeks? (*pp. 208-209*) _____
   _____

9. How do we determine that the 2300-year prophecy and the seventy weeks prophecy both have the same starting point? (*p. 208*) _____
   _____
   _____

10. What year did the seventy-weeks prophecy begin, and what year did it end? (*pp. 211, 209*) _____

Questions for Discussion:

1. With a prophecy so specific, why do you think so many Jews still rejected Christ?

2. When have you last heard a sermon on the seventy weeks prophecy or the 2300 days prophecy? Is this something we should hear more about?

Daniel receives one final vision that reveals the fate of his people

Daniel 10

Daniel's Final Vision

CHAPTER 10

1. In the third year of Cyrus king of Persia a thing was revealed unto Daniel, whose name was called Belteshazzar; and the thing *was* true, but the time appointed *was* long: and he understood the thing, and had understanding of the vision.
2. In those days I Daniel was mourning three full weeks.
3. I ate no pleasant bread, neither came flesh nor wine in my mouth, neither did I anoint myself at all, till three whole weeks were fulfilled.

CHAPTER 10

1. **Third year of Cyrus** - Around 536 BC, Daniel was about 88 years old and was near the end of his life. The prophet now introduces the final section of the book. Chapter 10 provides the setting for the prophecies found in chapters 11 and 12. **King of Persia** - Title for Cyrus. **A thing** - A unique expression used by Daniel that refers to his fourth and final prophetic revelation (This fourth prophecy spans chapters 10-12). Some believe that this fourth prophetic outline is a detailed explanation of events pictured symbolically in the "vision" of chapter 8:1-14. **Time appointed** - There seems to be some doubt about the exact meaning of this phrase. In the original language, this phrase often relates to war or conflict. The context of this verse may be emphasizing an intense struggle rather than a time period.
2. **Mourning** - Daniel does not give a reason for his mourning.
3. **Pleasant bread** - Delicacies. **Anoint myself** – Possibly relating to the use of oils that soothe the skin.

EG White Notes

CHAPTER 10

Upon the occasion just described, the angel Gabriel imparted to Daniel all the instruction which he was then able to receive. A few years afterward, however, the prophet desired to learn more of subjects not yet fully explained, and again set himself to seek light and wisdom from God. "In those days I Daniel was mourning three full weeks. I ate no pleasant bread, neither came flesh nor wine in my mouth, neither did I anoint myself at all. *SL 49*

The Clear and Present Paraphrase

CHAPTER 10

1. Daniel, who was also known as Belteshazzar, received one final revelation from God. This revelation was given to me in the third year of Cyrus, the King of Persia. This message was made clear to him, but there was a great struggle in order to understand.

2. This was revealed to me after I fasted and cried out to the Lord in prayer for three full weeks.

3. During this period, I ate no delicacies, no meat, or any rich foods. I did not drink any wine and even denied myself personal luxuries, such as fragrant oils, until the three weeks were over.

KJV Bible

4. And in the four and twentieth day of the first month, as I was by the side of the great river, which *is* Hiddekel;
5. Then I lifted up mine eyes, and looked, and behold a certain man clothed in linen, whose loins *were* girded with fine gold of Uphaz:
6. His body also *was* like the beryl, and his face as the appearance of lightning, and his eyes as lamps of fire, and his arms and his feet like in colour to polished brass, and the voice of his words like the voice of a multitude.

Daniel Commentary

4. **Four and twentieth day** - Depending on which calendar (Babylonian or Jewish), this date would be March or April of 536 or 535 BC. **Hiddekel** - A Hebrew name representing the Tigris River. However, we are not told where on the Tigris that this occurred.
5. **A certain man** - The heavenly being appeared in human form and closely resembled the description John gave of Christ in the Book of Revelation. No doubt, this was the same Individual. **Uphaz** - The location of the Uphaz is unknown.
6. **Beryl** - In the Hebrew, this is the word for Tarshish, which perhaps indicates where the product was obtained. **Lamps of fire** - Compare Revelation 1:14. **Polished brass** - Compare Revelation 1:15.

EG White Notes

Then I lifted up mine eyes, and looked, and behold a certain man clothed in linen, whose loins were girded with fine gold of Uphaz. His body also was like the beryl, and his face as the appearance of lightning, and his eyes as lamps of fire, and his arms and his feet like in colour to polished brass, and the voice of his words like the voice of a multitude" (Daniel 10:2-6). This description is similar to that given by John when Christ was revealed to him upon the Isle of Patmos. No less a personage than the Son of God appeared to Daniel. Our Lord comes with another heavenly messenger to teach Daniel what would take place in the latter days. *SL 49-50*

The Clear and Present Paraphrase

4. On the twenty-fourth day of the first month, I took a walk by the great Tigris River.
5. Suddenly I received a vision, and I saw Someone standing in the distance dressed in a white linen robe with a belt made of Ophir gold around His waist.
6. His whole body seemed to radiate with light, and His face was so bright it looked like a flash of lightning. His eyes appeared like a blazing fire, His arms were the color of highly polished brass, and His voice sounded like a large multitude of people speaking in unison. This was the Son of God!

7. And I Daniel alone saw the vision: for the men that were with me saw not the vision; but a great quaking fell upon them, so that they fled to hide themselves.
8. Therefore I was left alone, and saw this great vision, and there remained no strength in me: for my comeliness was turned in me into corruption, and I retained no strength.
9. Yet heard I the voice of his words: and when I heard the voice of his words, then was I in a deep sleep on my face, and my face toward the ground.
10. And, behold, an hand touched me, which set me *upon* my knees and upon the palms of my hands.
11. And he said unto me, O Daniel, a man greatly beloved, understand the words that I speak unto thee, and stand upright: for unto thee am I now sent. And when he had spoken this word unto me, I stood trembling.
12. Then said he unto me, Fear not, Daniel: for from the first day that thou didst set thine heart to understand, and to chasten thyself before thy God, thy words were heard, and I am come for thy words.

7. **Daniel alone** - The revelation was only given to Daniel, but those who were with the prophet felt the presence of a heavenly being.
8. **Remained no strength** - Compare Revelation 1:17
9. **Deep sleep** - To be benumbed.
10. **Hand touched me** - The hand belongs to the angel Gabriel. **Set** – "To set tottering." Even though Daniel was lifted from his previously collapsed position on the ground, his strength was still not such that he could support himself without trembling.
11. **Greatly beloved** - "Precious." Daniel was once again reassured of God's love for him.
12. **Fear not** - The angel reassured Daniel that God had heard him, and He was in control.

EG White Notes

The great truths revealed by the world's Redeemer are for those who search for truth as for hid treasures. Daniel was an aged man. His life had been passed amid the fascinations of a heathen court, his mind cumbered with the affairs of a great empire. Yet he turns aside from all these to afflict his soul before God, and seek a knowledge of the purposes of the Most High. And in response to his supplications, light from the heavenly courts was communicated for those who should live in the latter days. With what earnestness, then, should we seek God, that He may open our understanding to comprehend the truths brought to us from heaven.

...What great honor is shown to Daniel by the Majesty of heaven! He comforts His trembling servant and assures him that his prayer has been heard in heaven. In answer to that fervent petition the angel Gabriel was sent to affect the heart of the Persian king. The monarch had resisted the impressions of the Spirit of God during the three weeks while Daniel was fasting and praying, but heaven's Prince, the Archangel, Michael, was sent to turn the heart of the stubborn king to take some decided action to answer the prayer of Daniel. *SL 49-51*

The Clear and Present Paraphrase

7. I was the only one who saw Him, but those who were with me felt His presence, which was so powerful that they all ended up running away!

8. Despite being all alone, the vision continued, and I had no strength left in me.

9. However, I could still hear Him speaking. As He spoke to me, I was lying on the ground like I was in a deep sleep.

10. Then a hand touched me and helped me get up on my hands and knees, which by this time, were both trembling.

11. It was Gabriel, the angel. He reassured me by saying, "Daniel, you are highly esteemed by God, so I need you to stand in place and listen carefully to what I'm about to tell you." At this point, I stood to my feet, but they were trembling.

12. He continued, "Don't be afraid, Daniel. At the moment you started fasting and praying for understanding, your voice was heard, and that's why I'm here with you now.

KJV Bible	Daniel Commentary
13. But the prince of the kingdom of Persia withstood me one and twenty days: but, lo, Michael, one of the chief princes, came to help me; and I remained there with the kings of Persia.	**13. Prince** - In Hebrew, this is a word for chief, ruler, prince, or military commander. This may be referring to the literal King Cyrus or a demon that represented King Cyrus. **Withstood me** - We are shown a glimpse of the supernatural struggle going on between the forces of good and the forces of evil. **Michael** - Literally, "who is like God?" Michael appears to be the name of Christ before His incarnation. **One of the chief princes** - This expression can have multiple meanings. "Echad" in the original language can be translated as *One* or *First*. "Ri'shown" can be translated as *Chief*, but it's also translated as *beginning*, *eldest*, or *first in time*. "Sar" can be translated as *Prince*, *Captain*, or *Ruler*. With this understanding, verse 13 is better translated as, "One, who from the beginning has always been the Prince." **I remained** — Bible translations differ on the interpretation of this phrase. It's also unclear why the angel needed to stay if Michael had arrived. Considering the context, Michael was likely the one who stayed. **Kings of Persia** — "King of Persia."

EG White Notes

For three weeks Gabriel wrestled with the powers of darkness, seeking to counteract the influences at work on the mind of Cyrus; and before the contest closed, Christ Himself came to Gabriel's aid.

...All that heaven could do in behalf of the people of God was done. The victory was finally gained; the forces of the enemy were held in check all the days of Cyrus, and all the days of his son Cambyses, who reigned about seven and a half years. *PK 572*

The king of Persia was controlled by the highest of all evil angels. He refused, as did Pharaoh, to obey the word of the Lord. Gabriel declared, He withstood me twenty-one days by his representations against the Jews. But Michael came to his help, and then he remained with the kings of Persia, holding the powers in check, giving right counsel against evil counsel. *Lt 201, 1899*

The Clear and Present Paraphrase

13. The reason for the delay is that Cyrus, the Prince of the Persian Kingdom, fell under the influence of demonic powers and refused to cooperate with God's plan for your people. However, Michael, the One who was a Prince from the beginning, showed up and helped me. He also remained there with the Prince of Persia to keep those demonic forces in check.

14. Now I am come to make thee understand what shall befall thy people in the latter days: for yet the vision *is* for *many* days.
15. And when he had spoken such words unto me, I set my face toward the ground, and I became dumb.
16. And, behold, *one* like the similitude of the sons of men touched my lips: then I opened my mouth, and spake, and said unto him that stood before me, O my lord, by the vision my sorrows are turned upon me, and I have retained no strength.
17. For how can the servant of this my lord talk with this my lord? for as for me, straightway there remained no strength in me, neither is there breath left in me.
18. Then there came again and touched me *one* like the appearance of a man, and he strengthened me,
19. And said, O man greatly beloved, fear not: peace *be* unto thee, be strong, yea, be strong. And when he had spoken unto me, I was strengthened, and said, Let my lord speak; for thou hast strengthened me.

14. **In the latter days** - This expression doesn't always refer directly to the final events of history. This can also mean the final part of a particular period of time. **For many days** - The angel reveals to Daniel what would befall the saints throughout the centuries until the second coming of Christ.
15. **Dumb** - To be tongue-tied:—bind, be dumb, put to silence.
16. **Like similitude** - Gabriel veiled his brightness and appeared in the form of a human. **The vision** - Most likely the vision of chapters 10-12.
19. **Fear not** – This phrase is often used when God unveils the supernatural world to His servants (see Rev 1:17).

EG White Notes

So great was the divine glory revealed to Daniel that he could not endure the sight. Then the messenger of heaven veiled the brightness of his presence and appeared to the prophet as "one like the similitude of the sons of men" (verse 16). By his divine power he strengthened this man of integrity and of faith, to hear the message sent to him from God. *SL 52*

The Clear and Present Paraphrase

14. Now, I'll explain what will happen to your people in the coming days, which will extend to the end of the world."

15. While he was talking, I had a hard time keeping my head up. Eventually, my head slumped toward the ground, and I couldn't open my mouth to speak.

16. Then Gabriel, who had veiled his brightness in order to look like a man, came and touched my lips. At that point, I was able to speak again and said unto him, "I feel overwhelmed because I am so weak and powerless right now.

17. How can I ask you about what I've been shown when I can't even talk? Not only am I weak, but I'm even having a hard time breathing."

18. At that point, he touched me again, and I felt my strength returning.

19. Then he said, "Don't be afraid. You are highly precious in the eyes of God. Peace be to your soul and strength to your body." Then I responded to him and said, "Okay, now I'm strong enough to listen, please continue."

20. Then said he, Knowest thou wherefore I come unto thee? and now will I return to fight with the prince of Persia: and when I am gone forth, lo, the prince of Grecia shall come.

21. But I will shew thee that which is noted in the scripture of truth: and *there is* none that holdeth with me in these things, but Michael your prince.

20. With the prince - The angel is speaking of further conflict between himself and the Prince of Persia. **Prince of Grecia** - Just as powers of darkness contended for the mind of the Persian king, these dark powers would soon compete for the mind of the Greek king—Alexander the Great. Looking toward the future, the angel indicates that when he withdraws from the supernatural struggle, a revolution will ensue among the nations. While giving Daniel a glimpse of God's active control in world affairs, Gabriel reveals that the armies of Greece would soon sweep the world and destroy the Persian Empire.

21. Noted - "To inscribe," "to write down." **None that holdeth** - This phrase may also be translated, "there is no one who exerts himself." The probable meaning of the passage is that Christ and Gabriel assumed the special work of ensuring that Daniel received the prophecy of truth revealed in chapters 10-12. Chapter 12 confirms this idea as we see Christ returning as "the man clothed in linen" to ensure Daniel received the entire scripture of truth.

EG White Notes

Day by day the conflict between good and evil is going on. Why is it that those who have had many opportunities and advantages do not realize the intensity of this work? They should be intelligent in regard to this. God is the Ruler. By His supreme power He holds in check and control earthly potentates. Through His agencies He does the work which was ordained before the foundation of the world.

As a people we do not understand as we should the great conflict going on between invisible agencies, the controversy between loyal and disloyal angels. Evil angels are constantly at work, planning their line of attack, controlling as commanders, kings, and rulers, the disloyal human forces.

I call upon you who are not ready for the last great controversy to wake up.
Lt 201, 1889

The Clear and Present Paraphrase

20. Then he said, "Do you know, the only reason I came here was to ensure that you understood the vision? Now that you understand, I will return and continue working on the Prince of Persia; however, soon afterward, my attention will be on the coming Prince of Greece.

21. But first, let me show you what is written in the record of truth. Then, I will return, as I am the only individual who has been given the special assignment of ensuring that you receive this truth besides Michael, your Prince."

DANIEL 10 - TEST YOUR KNOWLEDGE

1. Approximately how old was Daniel when he received this vision? (*p. 220*)___

   _____

2. Who appeared to Daniel first? (*pp. 222-223*)_____

3. Whose hand touched Daniel? (*p. 224*)_____

4. Why was Gabriel sent? (*p. 225*)_____

   _____

5. Why did Michael come? (*p. 227*)_____

   _____

6. Name both possible identities of the Prince of Persia. (*p. 226*)_____

   _____

7. Who is Michael? (*p. 226*)_____

8. According to Ellen White, what conflict do we need to understand? (*p. 231*)__

   _____

9. Why did Gabriel have to veil his brightness? (*p. 229*)_____

   _____

10. Latter days can refer to the final events of history or_____

    _____ (*p. 228*)

Questions for Discussion:

1. According to Daniel and John the Revelator, the appearance of Jesus, prior to His incarnation, seemed to match His appearance post resurrection. Do you think his appearance in vision matched his appearance while He lived on this earth? If not, why?

2. Many Christians believe Michael was just an angel. Do you think it's important for all Christians to understand that Michael was Jesus?

3. Discuss the implications of Bible translators referring to Michael as "One of the chief princes."

Daniel is shown the two major powers that have always contended for control of the world—The King of the North and the King of the South.

Daniel 11

The Final War

CHAPTER 11

1. Also I in the first year of Darius the Mede, *even* I, stood to confirm and to strengthen him.
2. And now will I shew thee the truth. Behold, there shall stand up yet three kings in Persia; and the fourth shall be far richer than *they* all: and by his strength through his riches he shall stir up all against the realm of Grecia.

CHAPTER 11

1. **Also I** - This verse is a continuation of the angel's statement in chapter 10:21, so in reality, this is simply a continuation of Daniel 10. Gabriel reveals to Daniel that in the first year of Darius the Mede, he visited the king to "confirm and strengthen him."
2. **The truth** - Here is the beginning of Daniel's fourth revelation. Daniel 10:1 all the way to Daniel 11:1 is background and introduction to what is about to be stated. **Three kings in Persia** - The three kings that ruled after Cyrus were Cambyses II, Gaumata, and Darius I. **The fourth** - Xerxes, also known as Ahasuerus of the book of Esther, was the fourth king. **Far richer** - Xerxes was particularly proud of his riches (Esther 1:4). **Stir up all** - The divided Greek states began to unify against their common enemy under threat of inevitable defeat. In this fashion, Xerxes roused up all the realm of Grecia, which ultimately led to the demise of the Persian Empire.

CHAPTER 11

Daniel's prayer in behalf of his people, as recorded in the ninth chapter, was "in the first year of Darius" the Mede. Darius was favored of heaven; for in the first year of his reign the angel Gabriel "stood up to confirm and to strengthen him." *RH March 21, 1907*

Daniel's prayer had been offered "in the first year of Darius" (verse 1), the Median monarch whose general, Cyrus, had wrested from Babylonia the scepter of universal rule. The reign of Darius was honored of God. To him was sent the angel Gabriel, "to confirm and to strengthen him." Daniel 11:1. Upon his death, within about two years of the fall of Babylon, Cyrus succeeded to the throne, and the beginning of his reign marked the completion of the seventy years since the first company of Hebrews had been taken by Nebuchadnezzar from their Judean home to Babylon. *PK 556*

CHAPTER 11

1. Gabriel continued, "Which is also one of the reasons God sent me to strengthen and protect Darius during the first year of his rulership.

2. With certainty, here are the events that will happen in the future:
After King Cyrus is gone, three more kings will consecutively rise to power and rule the empire. Finally, a fourth ruler, named King Ahasuerus, will rise after them. However, Ahasuerus will have more wealth than any of them. He will use that wealth to build one of the world's largest armies and stir up all the Greek city-states to unify against the Persian Empire.

KJV Bible	Daniel Commentary
3. And a mighty king shall stand up, that shall rule with great dominion, and do according to his will.	3. **A mighty king** - Alexander the Great. **Great dominion** - Alexander had the largest empire the world had yet known.
4. And when he shall stand up, his kingdom shall be broken, and shall be divided toward the four winds of heaven; and not to his posterity, nor according to his dominion which he ruled: for his kingdom shall be plucked up, even for others beside those.	4. **When he shall stand up** - Alexander was at the pinnacle of his power when he fell suddenly ill and died. **Shall be broken** - Alexander left no successor, and his kingdom eventually fractured into four smaller kingdoms. **The four winds** - The four quarters of the compass. **Not to his posterity** - Alexander had a son, but he was killed while still a child; thus, no descendant of Alexander ruled.

EG White Notes

While Daniel clung to his God with unwavering trust, the spirit of prophetic power came upon him. While he was instructed of man in the duties of court life, he was taught of God to read the mysteries of future ages, and to present to coming generations, through figures and similitudes, the wonderful things that would come to pass in the last days. *YI, June 25, 1903*

Said a celebrated emperor when on his dying bed, "Among all my conquests, there is but one which affords me any consolation now, and that is the conquest I have gained over my own turbulent temper." Alexander and Caesar found it easier to subdue a world than to subdue themselves. After conquering nation after nation they fell,—one of them "the victim of intemperance, the other of mad ambition." *Good Health November 1, 1880*

The Clear and Present Paraphrase

3. But, a mighty king named Alexander the Great will rise to power in Greece. He will defeat Persia's last king, Darius III, and absorb his territory. Then, as the ruler of the former Persian Empire and unified Greek city-states, Alexander the Great will rule the known world, and no one will stop him.

4. However, at the height of his power, Alexander the Great will die suddenly. This untimely death will cause a frenzy among his generals and top officials, who will ultimately split the kingdom northward, eastward, southward, and westward. Alexander's son will also be assassinated before he can succeed his father, and the kingdom will be fractured into multiple territories. The Greek Empire will never be united as it was under Alexander the Great because all his top officials will tear the kingdom into multiple pieces, but only four of those pieces will be relevant.

5. And the king of the south shall be strong, and *one* of his princes; and he shall be strong above him, and have dominion; his dominion *shall be* a great dominion.

6. And in the end of years they shall join themselves together; for the king's daughter of the south shall come to the king of the north to make an agreement: but she shall not retain the power of the arm; neither shall he stand, nor his arm: but she shall be given up, and they that brought her, and he that begat her, and he that strengthened her in *these* times.

5. **King of the South** - This territory will vary, but at this point, it refers to Alexander's former general Ptolemy I Soter, who ruled Egypt in the south. **One of his princes** – Initially, Seleucus was a Babylonian governor, but in 316 BC, he was driven from his territory in Babylonia and placed himself under the command of Ptolemy, who helped him conquer the eastern region. **Strong above him** - Seleucus would later become stronger than Ptolemy and would be considered the greatest of the four kings from Alexander's divided kingdom.

6. **End of years** - About 35 years after the death of Seleucus I. **Join themselves** - A peace agreement, Antiochus II Theos (grandson of Seleucus I) divorced his wife Laodice and married Berenice, daughter of Ptolemy II Philadelphus. **King of the North** - The application of this term will somewhat vary as history unfolds, but here, it applies to Seleucus II whose territory was north of Palestine. **Neither shall he stand** - Antiochus was likely poisoned by Laodice. **Given up** – Laodice had Berenice and her son assassinated.

EG White Notes

From the rise and fall of nations as made plain in the books of Daniel and the Revelation, we need to learn how worthless is mere outward and worldly glory. *PK 548*

The Clear and Present Paraphrase

5. One of Alexander's former generals, Ptolemy I Soter, will become very powerful and rule Egypt as the King of the South. Later, a Babylonian governor named Seleucus I Nicator will arrive in Egypt seeking asylum. He will serve Ptolemy as a general, and Ptolemy will help Seleucus conquer Babylon and much of the eastern territory. This conquest will make Seleucus the King of the East, and he will become more powerful than Ptolemy. Later, Seleucus will defeat Lysimachus, the King of the North, in the Battle of Corupedium, making Seleucus the King of the North and East. Seleucus will be the greatest of Alexander's former generals and will rule the largest territory.

6. Conflicts will ensue between the northern and the southern territories, eventually leading to a peace treaty. To honor the treaty, Antiochus II, the then King of the North, will divorce his wife Laodice and marry Berenice, the daughter of Ptolemy II, the then King of the South. However, Laodice will end up poisoning her estranged husband, Antiochus, then murdering Berenice and her child.

7. But out of a branch of her roots shall *one* stand up in his estate, which shall come with an army, and shall enter into the fortress of the king of the north, and shall deal against them, and shall prevail:
8. And shall also carry captives into Egypt their gods, with their princes, *and* with their precious vessels of silver and of gold; and he shall continue *more* years than the king of the north.
9. So the king of the south shall come into *his* kingdom, and shall return into his own land.

7. **A branch of her roots** – In the Third Syrian War, Ptolemy III, Berenice's brother, invaded Syria for revenge. **Shall prevail** - Ptolemy III prevailed in his campaign against Seleucus II.
8. **Egypt** - The Ptolemaic dynasty ruled Egypt as the King of the South. **Their gods** - Ptolemy III recovered all the sacred images previously taken by the Persians and restored them to the Egyptian temples, from where they were taken. **He shall continue** - The literal translation is, "he shall stand." Many scholars believe this phrase means Ptolemy refrained from attacking the King of the North.
9. **King of the South** - Evidence suggests this scripture should be rendered: "He will come into the kingdom of the King of the South." In other words, after Seleucus II re-established his authority in the north, he marched against Egypt, hoping to retrieve his riches and regain his prestige. **Return into his own land** - Seleucus was once again defeated and returned to his own land empty-handed.

EG White Notes

The prophecies of Daniel and the Revelation should be carefully studied... *PaM 189*

The Clear and Present Paraphrase

7. Berenice's brother, Ptolemy III, who will at that time be King of the South, will hear of his sister's death and will raise an army to avenge her. During the Third Syrian War, he will attack Syria and be victorious against the then King of the North, Seleucus II.

8. Ptolemy III will also recover the sacred idols previously taken by the Persians. These, along with silver and gold, will all be taken back to Egypt. And though Ptolemy will be very successful, this will be the last time he will attack Seleucus II.

9. After some time, Seleucus II will recover from his previous defeat and will raise an army against Ptolemy III to regain the lost idols that were taken. However, Ptolemy will once again defeat Seleucus, sending him back to his home in the north empty-handed.

KJV Bible	Daniel Commentary
10. But his sons shall be stirred up, and shall assemble a multitude of great forces: and *one* shall certainly come, and overflow, and pass through: then shall he return, and be stirred up, *even* to his fortress.	10. **His sons** - Antiochus II's two sons, Seleucus II, and his half-brother, Antiochus Hierax. **Overflow, and pass through** – While Seleucus II was engaged in conflict with Ptolemy III, Seleucus' younger brother, Antiochus Hierax made himself ruler of Asia Minor, forcing his brother to turn his attention back towards the north to recover the lost territory from his brother. However, Hierax created an alliance and defeated Seleucus in the War of the Brothers. After the war, Hierax received word that his alliance created a conflict back home, so he returned to deal with his enemies.
11. And the king of the south shall be moved with choler, and shall come forth and fight with him, *even* with the king of the north: and he shall set forth a great multitude; but the multitude shall be given into his hand.	11. **Moved with choler** - In 217 BC, Ptolemy IV met Antiochus III near the Palestine-Egypt border in the Battle of Raphia. **Given into his hand** - Antiochus III was defeated.
12. *And* when he hath taken away the multitude, his heart shall be lifted up; and he shall cast down *many* ten thousands: but he shall not be strengthened *by it*.	12. **He** - Ptolemy IV. **Not to be strengthened** - Ptolemy slew thousands of Antiochus III's soldiers. Had Ptolemy continued, he may have become ruler of the whole kingdom, but Ptolemy failed to capitalize off his victory at Raphia and instead was only content in regaining what he had lost.

EG White Notes

...through Daniel were presented to the king things foretold in the prophecies concerning Babylon and other kingdoms. *7T 161*

The Clear and Present Paraphrase

10. Seleucus II will return to discover that his father's other son, Antiochus Hierax, has assumed control of Asia Minor. In order to take the throne from Seleucus, Antiochus will assemble an alliance of hostile nations and destroy Seleucus' army in the War of the Brothers. But, after his victory, Antiochus will learn that his alliance provoked a conflict back home, and he will be forced to wage war in his own territory.

11. Years later, the King of the South, Ptolemy IV, will lose territory to Antiochus III due to an act of betrayal. This betrayal will enrage Ptolemy and drive him to go on the offensive to attack Antiochus, the King of the North. These massive armies will clash in the Battle of Raphia, resulting in Antiochus' defeat.

12. After the war, Ptolemy IV will be so caught up in his success that he will miss the opportunity to wipe out his enemy for good. Even though Ptolemy will have destroyed thousands of Antiochus' men, his failure to pursue Antiochus will allow the northern king to rebuild his army. Ptolemy's failure will make his victory a temporary one.

13. For the king of the north shall return, and shall set forth a multitude greater than the former, and shall certainly come after certain years with a great army and with much riches.
14. And in those times there shall many stand up against the king of the south: also the robbers of thy people shall exalt themselves to establish the vision; but they shall fall.
15. So the king of the north shall come, and cast up a mount, and take the most fenced cities: and the arms of the south shall not withstand, neither his chosen people, neither *shall there be any* strength to withstand.

13. **Shall return** - Ptolemy V, the then King of the South, came to the throne as a child, presenting Antiochus III with another opportunity to seek revenge on Egypt. **After certain years** - Probably a reference to the 16 years between the battle of Raphia and Antiochus' second campaign against the south.
14. **Stand up against** - Economic troubles and high taxation led to seditions and uprisings in Egypt. **Robbers of thy people** – Literally, "*S*ons *of the oppressors*." Israel's first oppressors were Egyptian. The *sons of these oppressors* refers to the Egyptian insurgents who brought violence and bloodshed to the Ptolemaic Empire during a period of revolt. **They shall fail** - The insurrection ultimately failed after the death of, Chaonnaphris, the insurrection's leader
15. **King of the North** - Antiochus Epiphanes. **Fenced cities** - Literally, "a city of fortifications." A reference to cities that fell during Antiochus' campaign against the south. **Arms** - A symbol of strength, possibly an army or even the power behind the army—the king himself.

EG White Notes

Satan delights in war, for it excites the worst passions of the soul and then sweeps into eternity its victims steeped in vice and blood. It is his object to incite the nations to war against one another, for he can thus divert the minds of the people from the work of preparation to stand in the day of God. *Homeward Bound 344*

The Clear and Present Paraphrase

13. Years later, Antiochus III will return to invade and occupy Ptolemaic territories. However, the Ptolemaic commander will recapture these provinces, and Antiochus III will respond by assembling an even larger army than the one that previously fought at Rafah. Not only will he come back to the south with a larger army, but he will also have more battle equipment.

14. During that time, the King of the South, Ptolemy V, will not only receive threats from Antiochus III, he will also receive threats from his own citizens. In an attempt to overthrow their colonizers, fierce Egyptian insurgents will bring violence and bloodshed to the region during the Great Egyptian Revolt. These insurgents will rise with the hopes of ending Ptolemaic control over Egypt, but their insurrection will fail.

15. Years later, Antiochus Epiphanes will rise as the King of the North. He will nearly conquer all of Egypt as the Ptolemaic armies won't be able to stand up to him. Even God's Chosen people will be unable to defend themselves against him, and he will force them into false worship and persecute them.

16. But he that cometh against him shall do according to his own will, and none shall stand before him: and he shall stand in the glorious land, which by his hand shall be consumed.

17. He shall also set his face to enter with the strength of his whole kingdom, and upright ones with him; thus shall he do: and he shall give him the daughter of women, corrupting her: but she shall not stand *on his side*, neither be for him.

16. **He that cometh against him** - Rome was steadily rising to prominence and would eventually begin interfering in the affairs of the Seleucid Empire. **Stand in the glorious land** – Rome is the power that would ultimately occupy and destroy Jerusalem.

17. **Upright ones** - The meaning of this is obscure in Hebrew; however, this may be a reference to Jerusalem, which became a Roman province. **Daughter of women** - An unusual expression that may refer to Cleopatra VII as she was the most notable of the famous lineage of women.

EG White Notes

...much is said of Caesar and other great men of the world. Their exploits are recorded and sent through the length and breadth of the land; yet we have no evidence that these men honored God, or that God honored them. *RH April 15, 1909*

Read the book of Daniel. Call up, point by point, the history of the kingdoms there represented. Behold statesmen, councils, powerful armies, and see how God wrought to abase pride and lay human glory in the dust. God alone is represented as great. In the vision of the prophet He is seen casting down one mighty ruler and setting up another. *Christ Triumphant 335*

The Clear and Present Paraphrase

16. Unfortunately for Antiochus Epiphanes, the rise of the Roman Republic will stop him from fully conquering Egypt. The Romans will eventually come against the Seleucid Empire and defeat it. Rome will do as it pleases, and no one will be able to stop it. This nation will not only conquer the land of Israel, but it will also destroy Jerusalem and scatter its inhabitants.

17. Rome will focus on conquering the known world, including the children of Israel. During that time, Julius Caesar, a powerful Roman Consul, will be at war with another Roman Consul named Pompey Magnus. In pursuit of Pompey, Julius will go down to Egypt, where he will become involved with a daughter of the Cleopatrian family line—Cleopatra VII. Her father will place her under Roman guardianship which will lead to Caesar appointing her as the Queen of Egypt. However, power will corrupt her, leading her to kill her brother. Soon after, her life will end in tragedy. And even though she develops relationships with two Roman consuls, her loyalties will always remain with Egypt.

18. After this shall he turn his face unto the isles, and shall take many: but a prince for his own behalf shall cause the reproach offered by him to cease; without his own reproach he shall cause *it* to turn upon him.

19. Then he shall turn his face toward the fort of his own land: but he shall stumble and fall, and not be found.

20. Then shall stand up in his estate a raiser of taxes *in* the glory of the kingdom: but within few days he shall be destroyed, neither in anger, nor in battle.

18. **The isles** - "Sea lands" or "sea coasts." **A prince** - A man in authority, often a military commander. This individual most likely represents Decimus Brutus, who was like a son to Julius Caesar. **Reproach** – Brutus would cause the shame Caesar brought upon Rome to be brought back on Caesar.

19. **Stumble and fall** - Caesar was killed after returning to Rome by his own senators.

20. **A raiser of taxes** - Literally, "one who causes an oppressor to pass through," or "one who causes an exactor to pass through." The passage appears to be a reference to a king who would send oppressors or exactors throughout the realm. Most commentators have understood the reference here to be a tax collector, which was the very embodiment of imperial oppression. Luke 2:1 records one of Agustus' tax decrees, which occurred in 8 BC. However, the prophecy stated that he would die within a few days. History reveals that Augustus requested a final census in 14 AD. **Neither in anger, nor battle** – Soon after his last census, Augustus died peacefully in his bed.

EG White Notes

Alexander and Caesar found it easier to subdue a world than to subdue themselves. After conquering nation after nation they fell,—one of them "the victim of intemperance, the other of mad ambition." *Good Health November 1, 1880*

The decree of Rome to register the peoples of her vast territory had extended to the hills of Galilee. Caesar Augustus became God's agent to bring the mother of Jesus to Bethlehem. *Humble Hero 16*

The Clear and Present Paraphrase

18. After this, Julius Caesar will turn his attention to the Iberian Peninsula to destroy the remaining opposition forces led by Pompey's two sons. Once the opposition forces of Pompey are destroyed, Julius will believe he has put an end to all remaining opposition against him; but the war against Pompey will ultimately be the catalyst for Julius' downfall. His close friend Decimus Brutus will conspire with the Roman Senate to have Julius Caesar killed.

19. After Julius Caesar crushes his opposition, he will return to Rome, where he'll be elected dictator for life. However, the Roman Senators fearing that Julius' reckless use of power would be detrimental for them, will assassinate him.

20. Then Augustus Caesar, the great-nephew of Julius Caesar, will become Emperor of Rome. He will be known for imposing a great census upon the whole empire. However, a few years after this census is imposed, he will die. But, his death will not be in a murderous rage like his great-uncle. Instead, Augustus will die at an old age of natural causes.

KJV Bible

21. And in his estate shall stand up a vile person, to whom they shall not give the honour of the kingdom: but he shall come in peaceably, and obtain the kingdom by flatteries.
22. And with the arms of a flood shall they be overflown from before him, and shall be broken; yea, also the prince of the covenant.

Daniel Commentary

21. **A vile person** – One who is lightly esteemed, despised, or lowly regarded. Tiberius succeeded Augustus in 14 AD. Tiberius was a dark and reclusive ruler. In some sources, he was known as the "gloomiest of mankind." **They shall not give** - Literally, "they did not give." This reference is likely used because Tiberius was not originally in line for succession to the throne. Tiberius was not given the honor of the throne, but he received it because he was adopted. **Peaceably** - Tiberius ascended the throne without a war or power struggle. This can also mean prosperity. **Flatteries** - Most likely a reference to the fact that Tiberius obtained the throne through the maneuvering of his mother's marriage to Augustus, who adopted Tiberius as his son.
22. **Arms of a flood** - "Arms" denotes power, but here, specifically, military power. The picture portrayed is evidently that of flood-like armies of soldiers who destroyed Jerusalem in 70 AD. **Prince of the covenant** - This refers to Jesus, the Messiah, the Prince, who confirmed the covenant with Israel.

EG White Notes

By choosing a heathen ruler, the Jewish nation rejected God as their king. From then on they had no king but Caesar. The priests and teachers had led the people to this. They were responsible for this, with all the fearful results that followed. A nation's sin and a nation's ruin were due to the religious leaders. *Humble Hero 340*

The destruction of Jerusalem was involved in the Jews' crucifixion of Christ. The blood shed on Calvary was the weight that sank them to ruin. *Humble Hero 278*

Not one Christian perished in the destruction of Jerusalem. Christ had given His disciples warning, and all who believed His words watched for the promised sign. "When ye shall see Jerusalem compassed with armies," said Jesus, "then know that the desolation thereof is nigh. Then let them which are in Judea flee to the mountains; and let them which are in the midst of it depart out." Luke 21:20, 21. *GC 30*

After the destruction of the temple, the whole city soon fell into the hands of the Romans... *GC 35*

The Clear and Present Paraphrase

21. The next Emperor who obtains the Roman throne will be Tiberius Caesar. Tiberius will have a dark, reclusive personality and will later be known as the gloomiest man on earth. He will also obtain a bad reputation and will not be given the honor of a Caesar. In all actuality, the only reason Tiberius comes into the prosperity of the throne is through adoption, which will be manipulated by his mother through her marriage to Augustus.

22. Several years later, the Jews will seal their fate. The armies of Rome will overwhelm Jerusalem like a flood, destroying the city, the temple, and scattering its inhabitants. Understand that Jerusalem's desolation is a direct result of the Jew's rejection of the Messiah. Their rejection of Christ will lead Him to be crucified on the cross.

23. And after the league *made* with him he shall work deceitfully: for he shall come up, and shall become strong with a small people.
24. He shall enter peaceably even upon the fattest places of the province; and he shall do *that* which his fathers have not done, nor his fathers' fathers; he shall scatter among them the prey, and spoil, and riches: *yea*, and he shall forecast his devices against the strong holds, even for a time.

23. **After the league** – Daniel 11's underlying theme focuses on the conflict between the north and the south. However, at the height of Rome's power, it ruled both regions. After the destruction of Jerusalem, it is logical to believe that Daniel 11 skips over 400 years to focus on the next power to rise in the south—the Vandals. **League** - Possibly a reference to the 435 AD peace treaty made between the Vandals and Rome in which a portion of North Africa was ceded to the Barbarian tribe. The Vandals would later break that treaty and invade Carthage. **He shall come up** - The Vandals, from whom we get the term vandalism, were originally a small insignificant sect of people who became a mighty nation.
24. **Peaceably** - "Shalvah," in the original language. This word can mean *security* or *peacefully*, but it can also mean *prosperity*. North Africa was a very fertile and prosperous region of Rome. **Strong holds** - *Castle*, or *fortified city*. The Vandals captured Hippo Regius (modern-day Annaba, Algeria) and Carthage (modern-day Tunisia), which can be classified as essential cities that were well fortified.

EG White Notes

From the rise and fall of nations as made plain in the books of Daniel and the Revelation, we need to learn how worthless is mere outward and worldly glory. *PK 548*

The Clear and Present Paraphrase

23. Centuries later, Rome will begin experiencing an influx of Barbarian tribes invading from the north. The Vandal tribe, led by King Genseric, will sign a peace treaty with the Roman Empire; but this will turn out to be a big deception as the Vandals will break the treaty and continue attacking Rome. The Vandals will grow into a strong, powerful nation, even though they'll begin as a small insignificant tribe.

24. The Vandals will come into prosperity by taking the rich grain-producing lands of North Africa. King Genseric will also do something that none of his ancestors ever accomplished—he will take the wealth of Africa and distribute it amongst his people. The Vandals will also devise various schemes to raid and pillage other essential regions within the empire.

25. And he shall stir up his power and his courage against the king of the south with a great army; and the king of the south shall be stirred up to battle with a very great and mighty army; but he shall not stand: for they shall forecast devices against him.

26. Yea, they that feed of the portion of his meat shall destroy him, and his army shall overflow: and many shall fall down slain.

25. **Stir up his power** - Many provocations took place between the Romans and Vandals. This "stirring" began as soon as the Vandals took North Africa. **King of the South** - The Vandals were the first Barbarian tribe officially recognized as an independent country within Rome's territory. Because of the threat posed to the Roman Empire, the Vandals officially became Rome's rival to the south, or as Daniel called it— The King of the South. **Great army** – In 468 AD, Rome's Eastern and Western Empires combined forces creating one of the world's largest armies to invade the Vandalic Kingdom. **He shall not stand** – Rome would ultimately lose this war. **Forecast devices** – King Genseric's war tactics.

26. **They that feed** – King Genseric used Roman ships against the Romans after he captured a large portion of their fleet in a surprise ambush at the Carthage harbor. Many of Rome's captured Naval captains also switched allegiances and fought alongside the Vandals, contributing to Rome's defeat.

EG White Notes

There is need of a much closer study of the word of God; especially should Daniel and the Revelation have attention as never before in the history of our work. We may have less to say in some lines, in regard to the Roman power and the papacy; but we should call attention to what the prophets and apostles have written under the inspiration of the Holy Spirit of God. The Holy Spirit has so shaped matters, both in the giving of the prophecy and in the events portrayed, as to teach that the human agent is to be kept out of sight, hid in Christ, and that the Lord God of heaven and His law are to be exalted. Read the book of Daniel. Call up, point by point, the history of the kingdoms there represented. Behold statesmen, councils, powerful armies, and see how God wrought to abase the pride of men, and lay human glory in the dust... *TM 112*

The Clear and Present Paraphrase

25. Recognized by Rome as the new King of the South, the Vandals will continue to loot and plunder the Roman Empire. The destruction caused by the Barbarians will provoke Rome's emperors to send one of the largest armies ever assembled to destroy the Vandals once and for all. However, the Vandals will also rally their army to neutralize the threat posed by the Roman army. At the conclusion of this war, known as the Battle of Cape Bon, half of the Roman fleet will be destroyed, and thousands of Roman soldiers will be killed. Rome will ultimately lose this war because of the tactics employed by the Vandals.

26. You see, King Genseric will bribe top Roman officials to provide the Vandals with key military intelligence. He will even convince multiple Roman Navy captains to switch allegiances to him along with their ships. This is how the Vandals will often overwhelm Rome's armies and is also why Rome will lose many soldiers to them in battle.

27. And both these kings' hearts *shall be* to do mischief, and they shall speak lies at one table; but it shall not prosper: for yet the end *shall be* at the time appointed.

28. Then shall he return into his land with great riches; and his heart *shall be* against the holy covenant; and he shall do *exploits*, and return to his own land.

27. **Both these kings** – These two kings represent Hilderic and Gelimer. Hilderic was king of the Vandals. His cousin Gelimer was next in line for the throne. However, according to Gelimer, Hilderic was plotting to prevent Gelimer from succeeding him. Gelimer was also plotting to take the throne away from his cousin. Both kings sat at the same royal table plotting against each other. **Not prosper** – Neither plots would come to fruition. Gelimer would eventually kill Hilderic and become king, but his time on the throne would not last long. **Time appointed** – The set time.

28. **He** – Justinian I. **Return into his land with great riches** – After Justinian exhausted his country's treasury, he turned his attention to his subjects and over-taxed them. In this way, he returned great riches back to his land. **Against the holy covenant** – Justinian began giving the Bishop of Rome preference over the Christian Church. **Return to his own land** – Justinian tried to restore the empire to its former glory by reconquering territories that were taken by the Barbarian tribes.

EG White Notes

When the early church became corrupted by departing from the simplicity of the gospel, and accepting heathen rites and customs, she lost the Spirit and power of God; and in order to control the consciences of the people she sought the support of the secular power. The result was the papacy, a church that controlled the power of the State, and employed it to further her own ends... *1888 GC 443*

The Clear and Present Paraphrase

27. Years later, Genseric's grandson, Hilderic, will be the king of the Vandals. However, Hilderic will plot to stop his cousin, Gelimer from succeeding him, and Gelimer will conspire to take the throne away from Hilderic. Both the current king and the king-in-waiting will sit at the same royal table and pretend they are not plotting against one other. Unfortunately for them, neither king's plan will succeed as the Vandal's allotted time as the King of the South is about to come to an end.

28. Around this time, an emperor named Justinian I will inherit the Roman throne. However, after nearly bankrupting the kingdom, he'll begin confiscating his citizen's wealth in order to restore the nation's treasury. He will also declare the Bishop of Rome to be the head of all church affairs, which will eventually become an attack against the New Covenant. However, before all this happens, Justinian will have his heart set on retaking all the lands that were previously conquered by the Barbarian tribes. Justinian will begin this re-conquest campaign against the Vandals.

KJV Bible

29. At the time appointed he shall return, and come toward the south; but it shall not be as the former, or as the latter.
30. For the ships of Chittim shall come against him: therefore he shall be grieved, and return, and have indignation against the holy covenant: so shall he do; he shall even return, and have intelligence with them that forsake the holy covenant.

Daniel Commentary

29. **It shall not be as the former, or as the latter** - There were three major battles between the Romans and the Vandals: The first was called the Battle of Cartagena, which occurred in 460 AD. The second was called the Battle of Cape Bon, which was fought in 468 AD. The first two wars resulted in Rome's defeat; however, Rome's third major offensive against Vandals proved fatal for the King of the South. Because the majority of the Vandal fleet had sailed to eliminate the revolt in Sardinia, their borders were wide open for the invading Roman army.

30. **Ships of Chittim** - Ships of Carthage. Also a general term for islanders of the Mediterranean Sea. Clearly, these are references to the Vandals, who were known for their naval prowess. **Grieved** - The Vandal Kingdom ended in 534 AD when it was conquered by Justinian in the Vandalic War.

    Intelligence - In 533 AD, Justinian established the Code of Justinian. These laws gave power to what would later be called the Papacy, the power that would "...*forsake the holy covenant*."

EG White Notes

The accession of the Roman Church to power marked the beginning of the Dark Ages. As her power increased, the darkness deepened. Faith was transferred from Christ, the true foundation, to the pope of Rome. Instead of trusting in the Son of God for forgiveness of sins and for eternal salvation, the people looked to the pope, and to the priests and prelates to whom he delegated authority. They were taught that the pope was their earthly mediator and that none could approach God except through him; and, further, that he stood in the place of God to them and was therefore to be implicitly obeyed. A deviation from his requirements was sufficient cause for the severest punishment to be visited upon the bodies and souls of the offenders. Thus the minds of the people were turned away from God to fallible, erring, and cruel men, nay, more, to the prince of darkness himself, who exercised his power through them. *GC 55*

The Clear and Present Paraphrase

29. Remember, God has already determined when the Vandalic Kingdom will end. Therefore, at that designated time, the Roman armies will return to the south to destroy the Vandals. But this time, the war will not end in Rome's defeat as it did in the Battle of Cartagena, and the Battle of Cape Bon.

30. At that time, the Vandal fleet will be moving against Sardinia to neutralize the revolt. This diversion will allow Roman forces to bypass the Vandal fleet and engage the Vandal forces on land. At the conclusion of this conflict, known as the Vandalic War, the Vandals will be destroyed, and North Africa will be restored to the Roman Empire. However, around this same time, Emperor Justinian will also become more involved in matters of the Church and will begin enacting laws that defy God's holy covenant. Even though Justinian will be known for recovering a large portion of Roman territory, he will also be known as the one who will conspire with the Bishop of Rome to elevate him as the head of the Church.

KJV Bible	Daniel Commentary
31. And arms shall stand on his part, and they shall pollute the sanctuary of strength, and shall take away the daily *sacrifice*, and they shall place the abomination that maketh desolate.	**31. Arms** – Power, often denoted as military or political strength. **Sanctuary of strength** – Possibly, "The Sanctuary of the fortress." This phrase may allude to Rome, the religious headquarters of the Empire. Sylvester Bliss says, "The Pope was placed in quiet possession of the capital of Rome." *A Brief Commentary on the Apocalypse p. 169*. **Take away the daily** - The true church was persecuted and went into hiding (see commentary on chapter 8:11). **Abomination that maketh desolate** - An Abomination occurs when the holy is mixed with the profane. This Abomination first occurred when Rome besieged Jerusalem, but happened once again when Pagan influences infiltrated the holy grounds of the Christian Church. This infiltration of Paganism into Christianity began after the Bishop of Rome was given power from Justinian's 90-day ultimatum in which he "...published edicts in 538 AD compelling all to join the Catholic church in 90 days or leave the empire and confiscated all their goods." Dr. N Summerbell, *History of the Christian Church, pg.311*.

EG White Notes

In the sixth century the papacy had become firmly established. Its seat of power was fixed in the imperial city, and the bishop of Rome was declared to be the head over the entire church. Paganism had given place to the papacy. *GC 54*

Christians were forced to choose, either to yield their integrity and accept the papal ceremonies and worship, or to wear away their lives in dungeons or suffer death by the rack, the fagot, or the headsman's ax... Persecution opened upon the faithful with greater fury than ever before, and the world became a vast battle-field. For hundreds of years the church of Christ found refuge in seclusion and obscurity. Thus says the prophet: "The woman fled into the wilderness, where she hath a place prepared of God, that they should feed her there a thousand two hundred and threescore days." [Revelation 12:6.] *1888 GC 54*

The Roman Catholic Church has united paganism and Christianity... *Love Under Fire 232*

The 1260 years of papal supremacy began with the establishment of the papacy in A. D. 538... *1888 GC 266*

The Clear and Present Paraphrase

31. Once the Bishop of Rome is declared to be the head of Christianity, the Papacy will be established. Armies will enforce its policies; it will regain its seat of authority over the sanctuary in Rome; and Christianity, which is the continuation of Judaism, will be taken away and replaced by Catholicism, the Pagan-Christian mixture that results in ruin.

32. And such as do wickedly against the covenant shall he corrupt by flatteries: but the people that do know their God shall be strong, and do *exploits*.

33. And they that understand among the people shall instruct many: yet they shall fall by the sword, and by flame, by captivity, and by spoil, *many* days.

32. **Such as do wickedly** - Most likely a reference to those who adopted Catholicism, and possibly a direct reference to the line of kings who wore the crown as Holy Roman Emperors. **Flatteries** – Emperor Justinian confiscated non-Catholic property and gave it to Catholics. **People that do know their God** - Many Christians who saw the manipulations of the Papacy went into hiding. Groups such as the Waldensians and the Huguenots refused to let Rome control the dictates of their conscience, and the church went into hiding. The Church in hiding is also expressed in Revelation 12:14 - "And to the woman were given two wings of a great eagle, that she might fly into the wilderness, into her place, where she is nourished for a time, and times, and half a time, from the face of the serpent."

33. **They that understand** - Even though the majority of the Empire had fallen into apostasy, a small remnant of people understood the scriptures, and their eyes were open to the Papacy's deception. These individuals are called Protestant Reformers

Rome was not idle. Her emissaries hastened to Germany to congratulate the new emperor, Charles the Fifth, and by their flatteries, false representations, and protests, influenced him to employ his power against the Reformation. *ST August 2, 1883*

I was shown the Waldenses, and what they suffered for their religion. They conscientiously studied the word of God, and lived up to the light which shone upon them. They were persecuted and driven from their homes. Their possessions, obtained by hard labor, were taken from them, and their houses were burned. They fled to the mountains and suffered incredible hardships. They endured hunger, fatigue, cold, and nakedness...Many of their children sickened and died through exposure to cold, and the sufferings of hunger; yet the parents did not for a moment think of yielding their religion. They prized the love and favor of God far higher than earthly ease, or worldly riches. They received consolation from God, and with pleasing anticipations looked forward to the recompense of reward. *1892 Gospel Workers 57*

32. Emperor Justinian will corrupt many by rewarding all who convert to this religion. However, many will see through the Papacy's lies and preserve the knowledge of the truth, and God will strengthen them.

33. These individuals will expose Catholicism by teaching the truth from God's Word. Unfortunately, they and their followers will be persecuted for their faith. Many of them will be killed by the sword, some of them will be burned alive, and others will be held captive as if they are the spoils of war. This will continue for over a thousand years.

34. Now when they shall fall, they shall be holpen with a little help: but many shall cleave to them with flatteries.

35. And *some* of them of understanding shall fall, to try them, and to purge, and to make *them* white, *even* to the time of the end: because *it is* yet for a time appointed.

34. **Holpen with a little help** - 1517 AD is the year most scholars consider the beginning of the Protestant Reformation. Martin Luther nailed his 95 theses to the door of the Church in Wittenberg, Germany, protesting the sins of the Catholic church, and the movement took a foothold. This movement was the help that true Christianity was given during the dark ages of Papal domination.

35. **Time of the end** - The time that began in 1798 AD after Pope Pius VI was captured and the Papacy lost its supremacy.

EG White Notes

By a recent decretal an indulgence had been promised by the pope to all who should ascend upon their knees "Pilate's staircase," said to have been descended by our Saviour on leaving the Roman judgment hall and to have been miraculously conveyed from Jerusalem to Rome. Luther was one day devoutly climbing these steps, when suddenly a voice like thunder seemed to say to him: "The just shall live by faith." *GC 125*

The Protestant Reformers had built on Christ, and the gates of hell could not prevail against them. *GC 210*

The 1260 years of papal supremacy began with the establishment of the papacy in A. D. 538, and would therefore terminate in 1798. At that time a French army entered Rome, and made the pope a prisoner, and he died in exile. Though a new pope was soon afterward elected, the papal hierarchy has never since been able to wield the power which it before possessed. *1888 GC 266*

The Clear and Present Paraphrase

34. Even though many will die during this period of persecution, God will help them by raising up a reformer named Martin Luther. This theologian will challenge the actions of the Catholic Church, giving birth to a movement known as the Protestant Reformation. Though some of the princes will support this movement, many of them will be persuaded to continue clinging to Papal beliefs.

35. Those who follow Martin Luther's protest will be known as Protestant Christians. Many of these Protestants will fall. They will be placed on trial and executed, but they will also be made spotless in the eyes of God—especially during the 1260 years of persecution, which will end at the time it was prophesied.

36. And the king shall do according to his will; and he shall exalt himself, and magnify himself above every god, and shall speak marvellous things against the God of gods, and shall prosper till the indignation be accomplished: for that that is determined shall be done.

36. The King - The Papacy. **He shall exalt himself** - The apostle Paul employs similar language in his description of the Papacy when he says, "Who opposeth and exalteth himself above all that is called God, or that is worshipped; so that he as God sitteth in the temple of God, shewing himself that he is God." 2 Thessalonians 2:4. **Indignation be accomplished** - The 1260 years of Papal supremacy ended in 1798 AD after the Pope was captured by the French. Even though another Pope was chosen shortly afterward, it was quite evident that the reign of Papal supremacy was over.

The Pope of Rome has opposed and exalted himself above all that is called God or that is worshipped so that he sits in the temple of God showing himself that he is God. *Ms 115, 1894*

In the thirtieth verse a power is spoken of that "shall be grieved, and return, and have indignation against the holy covenant... *Lt 103, 1904*

Scenes similar to those described in these words will take place. We see evidence that Satan is fast obtaining the control of human minds, who have not the fear of God before them. *Lt 103, 1904*

The 1260 years of papal supremacy began in A.D. 538, and would therefore terminate in 1798. At that time a French army entered Rome and made the pope a prisoner, and he died in exile. Though a new pope was soon afterward elected, the papal hierarchy has never since been able to wield the power which it before possessed. *GC 266*

36. However, prior to its downfall, the Papacy will do whatever it wants. It will exalt and magnify itself as if it were Jehovah, thereby exalting itself above every other god. The Papacy will make blasphemous statements and laws against the God of gods and shall prosper until it is overthrown in 1798 AD. The Papacy's fall has already been determined by God and will happen exactly when He says it will.

37. Neither shall he regard the God of his fathers, nor the desire of women, nor regard any god: for he shall magnify himself above all.

37. Neither shall he - Considering the Papacy was overthrown in 1798 AD, the chapter appears to shift its focus to another power that had already taken over the south—The Ottoman Empire. **God of his fathers** – The Ottomans currently reside in Turkey. Many are not aware that when John wrote to the seven Churches in Asia (Rev 1:11), this was actually Turkey. This reveals that Jehovah was the God of the Ottoman's ancestors. **Desire of women** - Some commentators believe this phrase refers to the divorce law established by France. Others believe it relates to Catholic priests who were celibate. However, a discussion on marriage doesn't seem to fit within the context of this verse. Therefore, the desire of women likely refers to Mary, the woman who was desired by Catholics during the dark ages to the point where she was elevated to the Mother of God. **Nor regard any god** - Even though the Ottomans were Muslim, they did not force any of their conquered territories to convert to Islam. In this manner, they had no regard for any particular religion or god in their empire.

EG White Notes

Again and again at the critical moment the Turkish armies appeared on the frontier, or the king of France or even the pope himself made war on him. In this way, amid the strife and turmoil of nations, the Reformation had been left to strengthen and spread. *Love Under Fire 85*

The Clear and Present Paraphrase

37. But you should also know that during the Papacy's reign, another power will emerge. Turkish Muslims will rise and consolidate into a nation known as the Ottoman Empire. Even though their ancestors will be Christian, the Ottomans will have no regard for the God whom their fathers worshipped. They'll also have no regard for the veneration of Mary, the desired woman. In fact, they won't force those who they conquer to recognize any particular god as their priority will be on military conquests.

38. But in his estate shall he honour the God of forces: and a god whom his fathers knew not shall he honour with gold, and silver, and with precious stones, and pleasant things.

39. Thus shall he do in the most strong holds with a strange god, whom he shall acknowledge *and* increase with glory: and he shall cause them to rule over many, and shall divide the land for gain.

38. God of forces - Forces is also translated as a fortress, a fortified place, a fenced city. Considering the focus of this verse is the Muslim Ottomans who were often involved in Jihad, "the God of the fortress" can refer to the God of Mecca—Allah. **Knew not** – Considering Islam began in the 7th century, the Islamic God was unknown to the Ottoman's ancestors who likely worshipped Jehovah.

39. Strange god – Foreign god. To the Christians in Asia Minor, Allah would be considered a foreign deity. **Divide the land for gain** - The Ottoman Empire fell around 1840. Its territory was divided between the British and the French around 1919 AD through a treaty known as the Sykes-Picot agreement.

EG White Notes

We are to see in history the fulfillment of prophecy, to study the workings of Providence in the great reformatory movements, and to understand the progress of events in the marshaling of the nations for the final conflict of the great controversy. *LDE 15*

...the Turkish government would surrender its independence on the eleventh day of August, 1840. The prediction was widely published, and thousands watched the course of events with eager interest. At the very time specified, Turkey, through her ambassadors, accepted the protection of the allied powers of Europe, and thus placed herself under the control of Christian nations. *1888 GC 334-335*

The Clear and Present Paraphrase

38. But, in their territories, they will give preference to Allah—the god of Mecca. Though entirely unknown to their ancestors, the Ottomans will honor this deity in their mosques and temples decorated with gold, silver, and expensive ornaments.

39. The honor given to this foreign deity will be clearly acknowledged in Ottoman-controlled territories as it increases in glory and influence among the nations. The Ottoman Empire will expand and rule over many, but in the end, their Empire will fall and be partitioned to benefit other countries.

40. And at the time of the end shall the king of the south push at him: and the king of the north shall come against him like a whirlwind, with chariots, and with horsemen, and with many ships; and he shall enter into the countries, and shall overflow and pass over.

41. He shall enter also into the glorious land, and many *countries* shall be overthrown: but these shall escape out of his hand, *even* Edom, and Moab, and the chief of the children of Ammon.

40. **At the time of the end** – Time after 1798 AD. **King of the South** - The Ottoman Empire collapsed, but the Bible's reference to the King of the South reveals a possible future resurgence of an Islamic conglomerate of nations in the south. **King of the North** - Babylon consists of the Dragon (Pagan Rome), the Beast (Papal Rome), and the False Prophet (False American Protestantism). Since Pagan and Papal Rome had already fallen, the next and final phase of the Empire would logically point towards the United States of America. This nation is the King of the North and revives the Papacy.

41. **Glorious land** - Splendor. The glorious land is most likely the Land of Israel or possibly Palestine. **Edom, Moab, and Ammon** - In Deuteronomy 2:5,9,19, God commanded Israel not to bother these three nations as their land had been given to them as an inheritance. Today, these three tribes reside in the territory known as Jordan, and America will refrain from destroying them in honor of God's original command. Ammon means "chief" and represents Jordan's capital—Amman

EG White Notes

When the State shall enforce the decrees and sustain the institutions of the church, then will Protestant America have formed an image of the Papacy. *ST November 8, 1899*

But I have no light in particular in regard to what is coming on New York, only that I know that one day the great buildings there will be thrown down by the turning and overturning of God's power. From the light given me, I know that destruction is in the world. One word from the Lord, one touch of his mighty power, and these massive structures will fall. *RH, July 5, 1906*

We have no time to lose. Troublous times are before us. The world is stirred with the spirit of war. Soon the scenes of trouble spoken of in the prophecies will take place. *Lt 103, 1904*

We are living in the time of the end. The fast-fulfilling signs of the times declare that the coming of Christ is near at hand. The days in which we live are solemn and important. The Spirit of God is gradually but surely being withdrawn from the earth. *Welfare Ministry 134*

The Clear and Present Paraphrase

40. However, several years later, Islamic militants from the King of the South's territory will launch a terrorist attack against the King of the North—the United States of America. This assault, known as the 911 Terror Attacks, will result in airplanes crashing, skyscrapers crumbling, and thousands of people losing their lives. The United States of America will respond to this attack by launching a War on Terror. US forces will destroy multiple terrorist targets like a category five hurricane with tanks, Humvees, and many warships. America will attack many of the Middle Eastern countries by toppling regimes and setting up new ones.

41. Years after the War on Terror subsides, Islamic countries will launch a major attack against Jerusalem. This attack will prompt the United States to send its troops into this region of Palestine in order to defend Israel from its enemies. The United States and its allies will overthrow multiple countries in the Middle East, but Jordan will escape the onslaught as America will honor God's original command to spare them.

42. He shall stretch forth his hand also upon the countries: and the land of Egypt shall not escape.
43. But he shall have power over the treasures of gold and of silver, and over all the precious things of Egypt: and the Libyans and the Ethiopians *shall be* at his steps.
44. But tidings out of the east and out of the north shall trouble him: therefore, he shall go forth with great fury to destroy, and utterly to make away many.

42. **Countries** - Possibly the countries of the Middle East. **Not escape** – Unlike Jordan, there's no divine command forbidding attacks on Jerusalem.
43. **Gold and of silver** - It is possible that this refers to the literal treasures of Egypt or the actual economy of the country. **Ethiopians** – Ethiopia of Bible times would be located in southern Egypt and northern Sudan today. **Steps** - The figurative path that can be followed.
44. **Out of the east and out of the north** - If you recall, Seleucus I was the king of the eastern part of the divided Greek Empire. Seleucus would ultimately conquer the territory of Lysimachus at the Battle of Corupedium. In case you forgot, Lysimachus was the then king of Asia Minor, which was in the north. This victory made Seleucus the king of the east and the north! And now we can see the territory that was formerly part of the Seleucid Empire is the same part of the world that tidings will come out from and capture America's attention. Today these directions would essentially point us to Turkey and the Middle East!

EG White Notes

The world is stirred with the spirit of war. The prophecy of the eleventh chapter of Daniel has nearly reached its complete fulfillment. Soon the scenes of trouble spoken of in the prophecies will take place. *9T 14*

The Clear and Present Paraphrase

42. Egypt, however, will not escape. The United States and its allies will topple this regime along with others.

43. America will establish financial control over Egypt's wealth and its economy. However, Egypt will not be alone in its submission to the superpower. Libya and Sudan will also be forced to follow Egypt's footsteps and be under the control of the United States and its allies.

44. While all of this is happening, rumors of war will sound from Turkey and the Middle East. This threat will alarm America to the point that they will focus their war efforts against the whole Middle Eastern region. This war will be fought with great fury, and many will die as a result.

45. And he shall plant the tabernacles of his palace between the seas in the glorious holy mountain; yet he shall come to his end, and none shall help him.

45. Tabernacles - A tent, covering, or tabernacle. The word tabernacle was often used to describe God's sanctuary (see Exodus 33:9). **Palace** – A throne room or palace can denote a king's power. If we interpret "tabernacles" as a religious authority and "palace" as a political authority, we can see a power that encompasses both Church and State. **Between the seas** - Israel was located between the Mediterranean and the Dead Sea. **Glorious holy mountain** - Most likely a reference to Mount Zion, a hill in Jerusalem. However, the name is also used as a reference to the actual city of Jerusalem. **None shall help him** - Speaking of this same ending, Daniel 8:25 says - "but he shall be broken without hand." The powers of Mystical Babylon will ultimately be destroyed by the Hand of God, and no one will come to their rescue.

EG White Notes

Fearful tests and trials await the people of God. The spirit of war is stirring the nations from one end of the earth to the other. *Lt 119, March 1, 1904*

The prophecy in the eleventh of Daniel has nearly reached its complete fulfilment. Much of the history that has taken place in fulfilment of this prophecy will be repeated. *Lt 103, 1904*

The Clear and Present Paraphrase

45. At the conclusion of this war, the Papacy will emerge as a universal peace-keeping broker. The United States will then establish the Papacy's headquarters in Israel between the Mediterranean and Dead seas in order to prepare the world to receive Satan when he personates Jesus in Jerusalem. In the end, those who follow the lies of the Papacy and False Protestant Christianity will be destroyed along with Satan, and no one will be able to save them.

DANIEL 11 - TEST YOUR KNOWLEDGE

1. Who was the fourth king in Persia? (*p. 236*)_____

2. What country was ruled by the King of the South? (*p. 240*)_____

3. What verse in Daniel 11 introduces Pagan Rome? (*p. 248*)_____

4. What verse pertains to the crucifixion of Christ and the destruction of Jerusalem? (*p. 252*)_____

5. Which Barbarian tribe later became the King of the South? (*p. 256*)_____
   _____

6. According to Ellen White, the Roman Catholic has united _____ and _____ (*p. 263*)

7. What is the abomination that maketh desolate? (*p. 262*)_____
   _____

8. What year did the reign of the Papacy begin? (*p. 263*)_____

9. Who are the Kings of the North and South during the time of the end? (*p. 274*)
   _____

10. What happens at the conclusion of the final war? (*p. 279*)_____
    _____
    _____

Questions for Discussion:

1. Why do you think God used vague terms (King of the North and Kings of the South) to describe two opposing powers?

2. Do you believe the Islamic nations are part of Bible prophecy? Why?

3. How do you believe the world will end?

Daniel is shown three prophetic time periods.

Daniel 12

Three Prophetic Periods

CHAPTER 12

1. And at that time shall Michael stand up, the great prince which standeth for the children of thy people: and there shall be a time of trouble, such as never was since there was a nation *even* to that same time: and at that time thy people shall be delivered, every one that shall be found written in the book.
2. And many of them that sleep in the dust of the earth shall awake, some to everlasting life, and some to shame *and* everlasting contempt.

CHAPTER 12

1. **At that time** - This phrase indicates that the beginning of this chapter is a continuation of the vision that began in Daniel 11. We can now see that this vision led us to the most anticipated event in all of history—the Second Coming of Christ. **Michael** - See in chapter 10:13. **The book** - Book of life (see Daniel 7:10).
2. **Shall awake** - This awakening happens at the Second Coming of Christ. The righteous dead are resurrected; however, a special resurrection occurs for those who actively took part in the crucifixion of Jesus (Revelation 1:7). They will be raised to see Christ come in the clouds in all His glory, and then they will be laid back to rest until after the millennium. At the end of the millennium, all the lost will be raised from the dead to be judged and sentenced. Then God will send fire from heaven to destroy the wicked and purify the earth. This is called the second death (Rev 20:14).

EG White Notes

CHAPTER 12

...when our High Priest has finished his work in the Sanctuary, he will stand up, put on the garments of vengeance, and then the seven last plagues will be poured out. I saw that the four angels would hold the four winds until Jesus' work was done in the Sanctuary, and then will come the seven last plagues. These plagues enraged the wicked against the righteous, and they thought that we had brought them down upon them, and if they could rid the earth of us, then the plagues would be stayed. *The Present Truth 1849*

The world is becoming more and more lawless. Soon great trouble will arise among the nations—trouble that will not cease until Jesus comes. *LDE 12*

Graves are opened... "They also which pierced Him" (Revelation 1:7), those that mocked and derided Christ's dying agonies, and the most violent opposers of His truth and His people, are raised to behold Him in His glory and to see the honor placed upon the loyal and obedient. *GC 637*

The Clear and Present Paraphrase

CHAPTER 12

1. While the world is in a state of turmoil, Michael, the Great Prince, and defender of Israel, will finish His work as our High Priest in the heavenly sanctuary, and then He will stand up. At the moment He stands, the world will begin experiencing a time of trouble that will produce more devastation than any nation has previously caused. But God will save your people—those whose names are written in the Book of Life.

2. However, many of them, whose names are written in the Book of Life, will already be dead. So when Michael comes back to this earth, He will resurrect them from their graves. Most of the resurrected will be raised to receive everlasting life; however, those who had an active part in His crucifixion will also be resurrected to see Him sitting on the right hand of Power. They will see the Son for who He is, and they will experience shame and everlasting contempt for what they did.

KJV Bible	Daniel Commentary
3. And they that be wise shall shine as the brightness of the firmament; and they that turn many to righteousness as the stars for ever and ever.	3. **They that be wise** - Meaning "those who have insight." This is probably a reference to those who were persecuted for their faithful endeavors. Here, they are rewarded with eternal glory.
4. But thou, O Daniel, shut up the words, and seal the book, *even* to the time of the end: many shall run to and fro, and knowledge shall be increased.	4. **Shut up the words** - Compare the similar admonition Daniel was given in chapter 8:26. Seeing that many stories provided earlier in the Book are understood and have also been a source of blessing to believers, it appears that the command to "shut up the words" only applies to the portion of Daniel's prophecy that deals with the last days. **Run to and fro** – A phrase that describes a physical wandering or roaming about. Some commentators believe that this "running to and fro" describes the time that began after 1798 AD when many began searching the Word of God to understand Daniel's prophecies. **Knowledge shall be increased** - This is the logical result of the sealed book being opened at the time of the end, and knowledge concerning the truths contained in these prophecies increasing.

EG White Notes

When Satan shall have accomplished his work of ensnaring all who will subject themselves to his deceptive influence, when he shall have finished his work of scattering abroad, Christ will rise up and bring deliverance to every one whose name is found written in the book of life. Satan and his followers will be destroyed. Then "they that be wise shall shine as the brightness of the firmament; and they that turn many to righteousness as the stars for ever and ever." *Upward Look 365*

His wonderful prophecies, as recorded by him in chapters 7 to 12 of the book bearing his name, were not fully understood even by the prophet himself; but before his life labors closed, he was given the blessed assurance that "at the end of the days"—in the closing period of this world's history—he would again be permitted to stand in his lot and place. *PK 547*

...since 1798 the book of Daniel has been unsealed, knowledge of the prophecies has increased, and many have proclaimed the solemn message of the judgment near. *GC 356*

The Clear and Present Paraphrase

3. But those who know and teach the Word of God will reflect the light that exudes from Christ at His Second Coming. They will shine like a bright afternoon sky, and those who helped win souls to Christ shall glow like heaven's stars on a clear night. Their reward will last forever.

4. But Daniel, I want you to understand that the full explanation of these visions will be hidden and concealed until the time of the end, which will begin after the fall of the Papacy. During that time, many will become inspired to search for the meaning of these prophecies, and God will begin raising up men and women with the knowledge to understand them."

5. Then I Daniel looked, and, behold, there stood other two, the one on this side of the bank of the river, and the other on that side of the bank of the river.

6. And *one* said to the man clothed in linen, which *was* upon the waters of the river, How long *shall it be to* the end of these wonders?

5. **I Daniel looked** - Verses 1-4 conclude the vision given in chapters 10 and 11. Verses 5-13 seemingly refer back to the vision of chapter 8. This reference suggests chapters 10-11 are an explanation of chapter 8. **Other two** - Two additional heavenly beings appear here, joining the one who has been relating the prophetic events to Daniel. These two "saints" are possibly the same ones in chapter 8:13.

6. **Man clothed in linen** – This Man, who was also seen in chapter 10:5-6, was Christ. **Upon the waters of the river** – Notice, in chapter 8:16, the prophet "heard a man's voice between the banks" of the river. The visions of chapters 8 and 12 both refer to an individual who hovered above the river. **How long?** – In Daniel 8:13, the angel began his question by asking, "How long shall be the vision..." **Wonders** – A marvelous thing. Considering the context of the conversation and the fact that "wonders" typically refer to God's miraculous acts, these "wonders" are likely referring to God's miraculous power to make *knowledge increase* at the time of the end (vs. 4).

EG White Notes

The light that Daniel received direct from God was given especially for these last days. The visions he saw by the banks of the Ulai and the Hiddekel, the great rivers of Shinar, are now in process of fulfillment, and all the events foretold will soon have come to pass. *Christ Triumphant 335*

The book of Daniel is now unsealed, and the revelation made by Christ to John is to come to all the inhabitants of the earth. By the increase of knowledge a people is to be prepared to stand in the latter days. *2SM 105*

The prediction of Daniel, "Many shall run to and fro, and knowledge shall be increased," is to be fulfilled in our giving of the warning message; many are to be enlightened regarding the sure word of prophecy. *LT 12, 1907*

The Clear and Present Paraphrase

5. After this, the scene changed, and I saw two angels standing by the banks of a river. One angel stood on the river bank closest to me, and the other angel stood on the river bank that was on the other side.

6. Then, one of the angels asked Jesus, who was wearing linen garments and hovering over the river, "How long will it be until the end, when your power is manifested, and people begin to understand these prophecies?"

7. And I heard the man clothed in linen, which *was* upon the waters of the river, when he held up his right hand and his left hand unto heaven, and sware by him that liveth for ever that *it shall be* for a time, times, and an half; and when he shall have accomplished to scatter the power of the holy people, all these *things* shall be finished.

8. And I heard, but I understood not: then said I, O my Lord, what *shall be* the end of these *things*?

7. **Heard the man** – It appears that Jesus came to answer the specific question asked in Daniel 8:13—"How long shall be the vision concerning the daily sacrifice, and the transgression of desolation, to give both the sanctuary and the host to be trodden under foot?" **Time, times, and an half** – 1260 years beginning in 538 AD and ending in 1798 AD (For more information, see commentary under Daniel 7:25). **Scatter the power of the holy people** – God's people were persecuted for the duration of those 1260 years. **All these things shall be finished** – In the overall scheme of prophecy, all things will only be finished at the Second Coming; however, it's apparent that Christ was not telling Daniel when the world would end. Therefore, "all" must represent the persecution of the dark ages. In other words, Jesus revealed to Daniel that all these horrible things happening to God's people would be finished at the end of the 1260 years.

8. **I understood not** – Daniel was likely trying to understand how the time period related to Israel's deliverance.

EG White Notes

And now began the 1260 years of papal oppression foretold in the prophecies of Daniel and John.. Christians were forced to choose, either to yield their integrity and accept the papal ceremonies and worship, or to wear away their lives in dungeon cells, or suffer death by the rack, the fagot, or the headsman's ax. Now were fulfilled the words of Jesus, "Ye shall be betrayed both by parents, and brethren, and kinsfolks, and friends; and some of you shall they cause to be put to death. And ye shall be hated of all men for my name's sake." [Luke 21:16, 17.] Persecution opened upon the faithful with greater fury than ever before, and the world became a vast battle-field. For hundreds of years the church of Christ found refuge in seclusion and obscurity. *1888 GC 54-55*

The Clear and Present Paraphrase

7. Then I watched the Son of God, who was dressed in linen and hovering over the water. As He lifted both of His hands towards heaven, I listened as He swore by God the Father, who is immortal, and told me that these things would be allowed to continue for 1260 years, and then He will put an end to the hand that's crushing the holy people. This is when the persecution of the dark ages will be finished.

8. I heard what He said, but I couldn't understand how 1260 years correlated to the restoration of the sanctuary. So then I said, "My Lord, how will all of this end?"

9. And he said, Go thy way, Daniel: for the words *are* closed up and sealed till the time of the end.
10. Many shall be purified, and made white, and tried; but the wicked shall do wickedly: and none of the wicked shall understand; but the wise shall understand.
11. And from the time *that* the daily *sacrifice* shall be taken away, and the abomination that maketh desolate set up, *there shall be* a thousand two hundred and ninety days.

9. **Go thy way** - Daniel was not permitted to know the full understanding of the revelations he recorded.
10. **Be purified** - Purged. **Made white** – Cleansed, similar to an ethnic cleansing that occurs during the mass killing of a people.
11. **The daily sacrifice** - See comments on chapter 8:11, 11:31. **A thousand two hundred and ninety days** - This time period coincides with how long Pagan Rome would last from its inception. Rome was established in 753 BC by its first king, Romulus. The Pagan phase of this kingdom continued for exactly 1290 years until the transition to the Papal phase occurred in 538 AD.

EG White Notes

There is a work to be done in our world. "Many shall be purified, and made white, and tried; but the wicked shall do wickedly: and none of the wicked shall understand." The inability to understand is because of the strong unwillingness to confess and forsake error and accept the truth which involves a cross. Satan will strive to retain every soul in his strong power. He will not willingly let go his dominion over men who have influence upon other minds. Therefore God's own methods of advancing the gospel in his dominion are met by great opposition from the whole synagogue of the satanic agencies. As the last conflict with Satan will be the most decisive, the most deceptive and terrible that has ever been, so also will his overthrow be the most complete. *Bible Training School September 1, 1902*

"The wise shall understand" (verse 10), was spoken of the visions of Daniel that were to be unsealed in the latter days... *PK 547-548*

The Clear and Present Paraphrase

9. He responded and said, "This is as much as I am going to tell you, Daniel, because the meaning of this vision is hidden and concealed from understanding until the end of the 1260 years.

10. Until then, many will be persecuted, and attempts will be made to wipe the true believers off the face of this earth. Yes, the wicked will continue to do wicked things, but they won't understand what I've shown you. Only the wise will know the truth.

11. However, please know that when the time comes for Christianity, which is the continuation of Judaism, to be taken away and replaced by Catholicism, the Pagan-Christian mixture, 1290 years will have passed from the time of Rome's founding.

KJV Bible	Daniel Commentary
12. Blessed *is* he that waiteth, and cometh to the thousand three hundred and five and thirty days. **13.** But go thou thy way till the end *be*: for thou shalt rest, and stand in thy lot at the end of the days.	**12. Blessed is he that waiteth** – This blessing most likely applies to those who reach the Investigative Judgment of 1844. The prophet Isaiah says, "...for the LORD is a God of <u>judgment</u>: blessed are all they that <u>wait for him</u>" Is 30:18. **The thousand three hundred and five and thirty days** - Inspiration has provided us with all the time-relevant years in the Book of Daniel (457 BC, 538 AD, 1798 AD, and 1844 AD). However, none of these times coincide with the 1335 years. Considering the 1335 years are introduced after the 1290-year prophecy, it is logical to conclude that the 1335 years began after the 1290 years ended. Starting the 1335 years in 538 AD takes us to 1874 AD, but nothing prophetically relevant happened that year, which is why there should be some consideration that 1335 was not the original number. There is the potential that the copyist of the original manuscript wrote 1335, when it was originally 1305. Taking 538 AD and adding 1305 years to that date brings us to 1844—the year of the Investigative Judgment. **13. Thy lot** – Daniel would testify again through his visions.

Daniel has been standing in his lot since the seal was removed and the light of truth has been shining upon his visions. He stands in his lot, bearing the testimony which was to be understood at the end of the days. *Ms 50, 1893*

The Lord sent for the men to preach the message He should give them that Christ would appear the second time to punish the inhabitants of the earth for their iniquity in 1844. The time passed. The event anticipated did not take place. Yet the message of warning was of God, to test and prove the people of the world who heard the note of warning. The mistake was in the event. They were not in error in preaching time. God hid from them the event that was to take place. They thought Christ would come to this earth to purify the world by fire. They regarded the earth as the sanctuary to be cleansed at the end of the 1335 days. After the passing of the time, light shone more clearly upon the prophecies that the sanctuary to be cleansed was in heaven. Christ entered the heavenly sanctuary upon the great antitypical day of atonement to cleanse it from the sins of the people by virtue of His own blood. *Ms 6, 1876*

12. Even though God's people will be persecuted, He will ultimately vindicate them in the judgment. Therefore whoever faithfully waits and yearns for God to cleanse His sanctuary will be blessed when their name comes up in the judgment. This judgment will begin 1305 years after Catholicism replaces the Christian Church.

13. So go about the rest of your life until the time comes for you to rest in the grave. But be assured, at the appointed time, the prophecies you recorded will speak to those who will be alive during the time of the end.

DANIEL 12 - TEST YOUR KNOWLEDGE

1. What part of the Book of Daniel was sealed? (*p. 293*) _____

   _____

2. What event is happening when many that sleep awaken? (*p. 284*) _____

   _____

3. What happens on earth after Jesus finishes His work in the heavenly sanctuary? (*p. 285*) _____

4. Who was the Man clothed in linen? (*p. 288*) _____

5. When did the Book of Daniel become an unsealed book? (*p. 287*) _____

6. What chapter did Daniel previously record a vision in which Christ hovered over a river? (*p. 288*) _____

7. Daniel was told he would stand in his lot at the end of days. What did this mean? (*p. 294*) _____

   _____

8. When did the 1290-day prophecy begin and end? (*p. 292*) _____

9. What special group is raised at the Second Coming? (*p. 285*) _____

   _____

10. What began at the end of the 1335 days? (*p. 294*) _____

    _____

Questions for Discussion:

1. Discuss other possible start and end times for the 1290 and 1335-day prophecies.

2. Can a case be made that the daily being taken away was the taking away of Paganism in 508 AD?

3. Why are those who pierced Jesus going to be raised at Jesus Second Coming?

4. Are you ready for Michael to stand up?

THE DANIEL PARALLEL
A Clear and Present Truth Reference Guide

Test Your Knowledge Questions and Answers

TEST YOUR KNOWLEDGE QUESTIONS AND ANSWERS

Daniel 1
1. What were the three Hebrew boys' original names? **Hananiah Mishael and Azariah.**
2. Who was the Master of the eunuchs? **Ashpenaz**
3. Why did God give Daniel favor with the prince of the eunuchs? **He kept before him the fear of the Lord.**
4. What is the meaning of Daniel's name? **God is my judge.**
5. Who was the king of Judah when Nebuchadnezzar besieged it? **Jehoiakim**
6. True or **False** - The only issue with the king's meat is that it was un-clean.
7. What is pulse? **Food derived from plants.**
8. Who was the chief god of the Babylonians? **Marduk**
9. How many days was Daniel given to prove his diet was superior to the king's diet? **Ten days**
10. What was Daniel's Babylonian name? **Belteshazzar**

Daniel 2
1. Who did King Nebuchadnezzar call upon first in order to interpret his dream? **Magicians, and the astrologers, and the sorcerers, and the Chaldeans.**
2. What did the king mean when he said, "I know of certainty that ye would gain the time?" **The wise men would try to buy time or stall for more time.**
3. What was Daniel's first act after God revealed the interpretation of the king's dream to him? **He blessed the God of heaven.**
4. Name all the elements of the image Nebuchadnezzar saw. **Gold, silver, brass, iron, iron mixed with clay.**
5. What hit the image and broke it into pieces? **A stone.**
6. Name each element of the image and the nation that it correlates to. **Gold - Babylon, Silver - Media-Persia, Brass - Greece, Iron - Rome, Clay - Papal Rome**
7. How does Ellen White further describe iron and clay? **The mingling of church craft and state craft is represented by the iron and the clay.**
8. True or False - Religion and morality deteriorated more and more with the succession of each world power. **True**
9. According to Jeremiah 51:7, to what does God compare Babylon? **A golden cup.**
10. What part of the image pertains to the kings of the earth? **The ten toes.**

Daniel 3
1. What did the statue made of all gold represent to Nebuchadnezzar? **Babylon's eternal glory.**
2. True or **False**: The Jews were exempt from having to bow to the image?
3. What was the motive behind Nebuchadnezzar's wise men informing him that the Hebrew had defied his orders? **They were jealous of the honors that had been bestowed upon Daniel.**
4. Why did the king make the fire seven times hotter? **He felt that it required more than ordinary power to deal with the Hebrews**
5. True or False - Gabriel showed up in the fire with the three Hebrew boys. **False, it was Christ.**
6. How did Nebuchadnezzar know about the Son of God? **Through the Hebrew's testimony.**
7. What happened to the men that threw the Hebrew boys into the fire? **They died.**

Test Your Knowledge Questions and Answers

8. After Nebuchadnezzar's dream was revealed to him, he was initially influenced by the fear of God. Why did he change? **His heart was not yet cleansed from worldly ambition and a desire for self-exaltation.**
9. Whose attributes made Nebuchadnezzar's countenance appear like a demon? **Satanic**
10. Ellen White says, "God never compels the **obedience** of a man.

Daniel 4
1. What was behind Nebuchadnezzar's spirit of jealously? **The kingdoms that would come after Babylon.**
2. Who did the tree represent? **King Nebuchadnezzar**
3. Who did Nebuchadnezzar first call after his dream? **The Wise men of Babylon.**
4. Where was Nebuchadnezzar when he had this vision/ dream? **His house**
5. Explain what Nebuchadnezzar saw in his dream? **Read Daniel 4:10-17.**
6. What was Daniel's reaction when he understood the meaning of the king's vision/ dream? **Astonishment**
7. How many years was Nebuchadnezzar to dwell with the beasts of the field? **Seven years**
8. What did God want Nebuchadnezzar to realize before he would be reinstated as king? **The most High ruleth in the kingdom of men, and giveth it to whomsoever he will.**
9. Why did Daniel tell the king to break off his sins? **To prevent the foreseen tragedy**
10. What does Nebuchadnezzar say God is able to do to those who walk in pride? **Abase**

Daniel 5
1. What is the meaning of MENE, MENE, TEKEL, UPHARSIN? **God hath numbered thy kingdom, and finished it, Thou art weighed in the balances, and art found wanting, Thy kingdom is divided, and given to the Medes and Persians.**
2. True or **False** - Belshazzar was ignorant of Nebuchadnezzar's experiences with the God of heaven.
3. True or **False** - Belshazzar was the son of King Nebuchadnezzar.
4. What did Belshazzar order to be brought to the party? **The golden and silver vessels from the temple.**
5. Why did Daniel replace the word *Peres* with the word *Upharsin* in his explanation of the handwriting? **So Belshazzar would know that Babylon was to be broken into two pieces.**
6. What happened during the party that frightened Belshazzar? **He saw a hand writing on the wall.**
7. What was happening outside the city gates while Belshazzar partied? **The Medes and Persians were marching into the heart of the city.**
8. Who suggested that Daniel be summoned to interpret the writing on the wall? **The queen.**
9. Belshazzar offered Daniel the third-highest position in the kingdom of Babylon. Who occupied the first two positions? **Belshazzar's father, Nabonidus, then Belshazzar**
10. What was the name of the king that took the kingdom from Belshazzar? **Darius the Mede.**

Daniel 6
1. What proclamation was made by Darius after Daniel was freed from the lion's den? **That in every dominion of my kingdom men tremble and fear before the God of Daniel.**
2. How many princes did Darius set over the Kingdom of Babylon? **120 princes**

303

TEST YOUR KNOWLEDGE QUESTIONS AND ANSWERS

3. Why was the lion's den sealed? **Guaranteed Daniel would not be rescued or killed by other means.**
4. Why was Daniel preferred over the other princes? **An excellent spirit *was* in him.**
5. What did Darius attempt to do once he realized Daniel would have to die? **He looked for a way to free Daniel.**
6. Why did the princes attempt to use God's law against Daniel? **They could find no fault in him.**
7. How many times per day did Daniel have prayer? **Three times**
8. Why didn't Darius change the law in favor of Daniel? **The Median and Persian law was unchangeable.**
9. What did Daniel say to Darius to proclaim his innocence? **Forasmuch as before him innocency was found in me; and also before thee, O king, have I done no hurt.**
10. How were the princes that tried to destroy Daniel punished? **They were cast into the den of lions with their families.**

Daniel 7

1. What do the four winds of Daniel's vision represent? **Conquest and Revolution**
2. What are the four beasts and the nations that each represent? **Lion - Babylon, Bear - Media-Persia, Leopard - Greece, Terrible beast – Rome.**
3. What do the three ribs in the bear's mouth represent? **The destruction of the three world empires that preceded it. (Egypt, Assyria, and Babylon).**
4. What was the meaning of the Bear being raised on one side? **Persia would one day dominate Media.**
5. Who do the ten horns represent? **Egyptian Kings, Assyrian Kings, Babylonian Kings, Median Kings, Persian Kings, Greek King, Asia-Minor Kings (north), Ptolemaic Kings (south), Seleucid Kings (east), Macedonian Kings (west)**
6. Who is the Little Horn? **Pagan Rome's kings and Papal Rome's Popes.**
7. Who is the Ancient of Days? **God Almighty**
8. Who were the three horns destroyed by the Little Horn? **Macedonia Kings in the west, Seleucia Kings in the east, and Ptolemaic Kings in the south.**
9. Explain how the Little Horn impacted the seventh-day Sabbath. **The Papacy has made the whole Christian world believe the Sabbath has been changed to Sunday. Most Christians follow this tradition to this day.**
10. Explain the meaning of a time, times, and the dividing of time. **Time - 360 years, times - 720 years, dividing of time - 180 years.**

Daniel 8

1. Who is the Prince of the Host? **Jesus**
2. What nation did the ram with two horns represent? **Media-Persia**
3. Explain why one horn was higher than the other. **Persia became the dominant power.**
4. Explain the cleansing of the sanctuary. **Also known as the Day of Atonement, this was the one day out of the year that the sanctuary was freed or cleansed from the sins of the people. The earthly sanctuary is a model of the heavenly sanctuary, so the same thing that happened in the earthly sanctuary takes place in the heavenly.**
5. What nation was represented by the goat? **Greece**
6. Explain what happened when the goat's horn was broken. **Alexander the Great died suddenly.**

TEST YOUR KNOWLEDGE QUESTIONS AND ANSWERS

7. Explain how the 2300-day prophecy refers to years and not days. **Utilize the year-for-a-day principle.**
8. What are the two classes of this world? **Those who worship God and keep His commandments, and those who worship the beast and his image.**
9. Explain the Daily Sacrifice. *Sacrifice* **is not in the original manuscript, and** *Daily* **means continual. The** *continual* **is the CONTINUATION of Israel, known as the New Testament Church.**
10. What marked the beginning of the Dark Ages? **The accession of the Roman Church to power.**

Daniel 9
1. According to Daniel, how many years were the Jews to be held in captivity? **Seventy years**
2. What book of the Old Testament did Daniel read? **Jeremiah**
3. Who showed up while Daniel was praying? **Gabriel**
4. What did Daniel need help understanding? **The relation between the 70 years captivity and the 2300 days (years)**
5. Using the day for a year principle, how many years is seventy weeks? **490 years**
6. What happened in the middle of the 70th week? **Christ was crucified.**
7. Explain what event, Gabriel told Daniel, would indicate the starting point for the seventy weeks prophecy? **The commandment to restore and build Jerusalem.**
8. What even marked the end of the seventy weeks? **The stoning of Stephen.**
9. How do we determine that both the 2300-day prophecy and the seventy weeks prophecy have the same starting point? **The 2300-year prophecy from chapter 8 has no starting point. When we view chapter 9, we see the 70 weeks are determined. Determined in the original language means "to cut" or "to cut off." Since chapter 9 appears to be an exposition of the unexplained portion of the vision in chapter 8, it is logical to conclude that the 70 weeks or 490 years were to be "cut off" from the longer 2300-day (year) period, which means they both would have the same starting point.**
10. What year did the seventy weeks prophecy begin, and what year did it end? **457 BC - 34 AD**

Daniel 10
1. Approximately how old was Daniel when he received this vision? **88 years old**
2. Who appeared to Daniel first? **Jesus Christ**
3. Whose hand touched Daniel? **Gabriel**
4. Why was Gabriel sent? **Gabriel was sent to affect the heart of the Persian king.**
5. Why did Michael come? **To help Gabriel counteract the influences working on Cyrus' mind.**
6. Name both possible identities of the Prince of Persia. **The literal King Cyrus, or a demon that represented King Cyrus.**
7. Who is Michael? **Christ**
8. According to Ellen White, what conflict do we need to understand? **The conflict going on between invisible agencies, the controversy between loyal and disloyal angels.**
9. Why did Gabriel have to veil his brightness? **His divine glory was too much for Daniel.**
10. Latter days can refer to the final events of history or <u>**the final part of a period of time.**</u>

Test Your Knowledge Questions and Answers

Daniel 11
1. Who was the fourth king in Persia? **Xerxes**
2. What country was ruled by the King of the South? **Egypt**
3. What verse in Daniel 11 introduces Pagan Rome? **Verse 16**
4. What verse pertains to the crucifixion of Christ and the destruction of Jerusalem? **Verse 22**
5. Which Barbarian tribe later became the King of the South? **Vandals**
6. According to Ellen White, the Roman Catholic has united **Paganism** and **Christianity**.
7. What is the abomination that maketh desolate? **When Pagans or Gentiles venture onto God's Holy ground. Paganism entered Christianity and formed an organization known as the Papacy; this is the Abomination of Desolation.**
8. What year did the reign of the Papacy begin? **538 AD**
9. Who are the Kings of the North and South during the time of the end? **The King of the North is the United States pushed by the Papacy, and the King of the South is an Islamic confederation of countries.**
10. What happens at the conclusion of the final war? **The Papacy will obtain a presence in Palestine by planting its headquarters in Jerusalem.**

Daniel 12
1. What part of the Book of Daniel was sealed? **His visions.**
2. What event is happening when many that sleep awaken? **Second Coming of Christ and the Resurrection.**
3. What happens on earth after Jesus finishes His work in the heavenly sanctuary? **The Seven Last Plagues begin.**
4. Who was the Man clothed in linen? **Christ**
5. When did the Book of Daniel become an unsealed book? **1798**
6. What chapter did Daniel previously record a vision in which Christ hovered over a river? **Daniel 8**
7. Daniel was told he would stand in his lot at the end of days. What did this mean? **He would once again testify through his prophecies.**
8. When did the 1290-day prophecy begin and end? **753 BC - 538 AD**
9. What special group is raised at the Second Coming? **Those who crucified Christ.**
10. What began at the end of the 1335 days? **The Investigative Judgment.**

Topical Index

1260 days, 162, 268, 269
1290 days, 292
1305 days, *See* 1335
1335 days, 294
1798 (year), 162, 268, 269, 270, 287, 294
1844 Judgment, 177, 180, 181, 294
2300 days, 180, 181
457 (year), 180, 210, 211, 294
538 (year), 162, 262, 269, 292, 294
A time (prophetic), 162
Abednego (meaning), 18
Abomination that maketh desolate, 262
Africa, 254, 255, 256, 261
Alexander the Great, 144, 145, 172, 184, 185, 238
Ancient of days, 150, 151, 152, 158
Babylon, 16, 17, 22, 23, 29, 32, 33, 34, 35, 36, 37, 42, 43, 45, 48, 49, 54, 55, 57, 58, 59, 61, 65, 68, 69, 74, 75, 77, 81, 86, 87, 96, 97, 98, 101, 102, 103, 110, 111, 112, 113, 132, 140, 141, 142, 143, 153, 171, 185, 196, 197, 245, 276
Babylonia, 16, 17, 96
Bear (kingdom), 142
Belteshazzar, (meaning 18), 19, 36, 76, 77, 80, 81, 82, 83, 102, 103, 220, 221
Book of life, 151
Brass, 40, 41, 44, 48, 49, 80, 84, 85, 96, 97, 108, 156, 222, 223
Chaldeans, 16, 19, 28, 29, 30, 42, 55, 56, 57, 58, 59, 60, 76, 77, 98, 100, 101, 112, 113, 196
Clay, 40, 41, 44, 45, 46, 47, 48, 49, 50
Covenant, 179, 196, 197, 214, 252, 264
Cyrus, 22, 23, 111, 112, 113, 134, 135, 170, 185, 196, 220, 221, 227, 236, 237, 276
Daily sacrifice, 176
Darius the Mede, 111, 113, 196, 236
Day of Atonement, 180, 181, 183
Decree, 30, 32, 33, 49, 58, 59, 68, 69, 74, 80, 84, 85, 97, 122, 124, 125, 126, 130, 132, 133, 162, 210, 211, 250
Destruction of Jerusalem, 253
Edom, Moab, and Ammon, 274
Egypt, 75, 98, 142, 143, 170, 202, 203, 240, 242, 243, 246, 247, 249, 276, 277
Evening and the morning, 190

Fiery furnace, 56
Fourth beast (kingdom), 146
Fourth kingdom, 44
Gabriel, 182, 183, 185, 190, 206, 207, 209, 221, 224, 225, 227, 228, 229, 230, 236, 237
Glorious land, 274
God of forces, 272
Gold, 40, 41, 42, 44, 45, 48, 49, 54, 55, 70, 96, 97, 98, 99, 104, 105, 108, 109, 112, 113, 142, 222, 223, 242, 243, 272, 273, 276
Greece, 44, 45, 143, 153, 160, 161, 172, 185, 187, 230, 231, 237, 239
Iron, 40, 41, 44, 45, 46, 47, 48, 49, 50, 80, 81, 84, 85, 96, 97, 108, 109, 146, 147, 156
Jerusalem, 16, 17, 96, 97, 109, 122, 123, 174, 178, 180, 187, 196, 197, 198, 199, 202, 203, 204, 205, 207, 209, 210, 211, 212, 213, 215, 248, 249, 252, 253, 254, 262, 267, 275, 276, 278, 279, 280
Judgment, 150
King of the North, 240, 242, 243, 245, 274, 275
King of the South, 242, 247, 256, 260, 274
Leopard (king), 144
Lion (empire), 142
Little horn, 148
Luther. *See* Martin Luther
LXX (definition), 28
Martin Luther, 266, 267
Medes, 42, 44, 45, 110, 111, 113, 120, 122, 124, 125, 126, 132, 170, 196, 197, 276
Medo-Persia, 44, 45, 143, 153
Melzar, 20
MENE, MENE, TEKEL, UPHARSIN, 108
Meshach, 18, 19, 48, 49, 58, 59, 60, 61, 62, 63, 64, 65, 66, 67, 68, 69
Michael, 225, 226, 227, 230, 231, 284, 285
Nabonidus, 97, 98, 112
Nebuchadnezzar, 16, 17, 19, 22, 23, 28, 29, 31, 32, 33, 35, 36, 37, 38, 39, 42, 43, 47, 48, 49, 54, 55, 56, 57, 58, 59,

60, 61, 62, 63, 64, 65, 66, 67, 68, 69, 74, 75, 77, 80, 81, 82, 83, 86, 87, 88, 89, 90, 91, 96, 97, 100, 101, 102, 103, 106, 107, 109, 126, 142
New York, 275
Nimrod, 42, 86
Palestine, 240, 248, 274
Papacy, 175, 259, 263
Persians, 42, 45, 110, 111, 113, 120, 122, 124, 125, 126, 196, 211, 242, 243, 276
Prince of the host, 176
Protestant Reformation, 266
Rome, 44, 45, 47, 143, 146, 148, 149, 152, 153, 158, 159, 160, 161, 162, 163, 171, 174, 176, 178, 185, 186, 187, 188, 189, 215, 248, 249, 250, 251, 253, 254, 255, 256, 257, 258, 259, 260, 261, 262, 263, 264, 265, 267, 269, 274, 280, 292, 293
Sabbath, 162, 163

Second Coming, 38, 284
Seventy weeks, 208
Shadrach (meaning), 18
Ships of Chittim, 260
Silver, 40, 41, 44, 45, 48, 49, 96, 97, 108, 109, 113, 142, 242, 243, 272, 273, 276
Son of God, 64, 65, 152, 189, 223, 261
Son of man, 152
Ten horns, 146
Three of the first horns, 148
Time of the end, 182, 266
Transgression of desolation, 178
United States, 46, 274, 275, 277, 279,
Vandals, 254, 255, 256, 257, 260, 261
Winds, 140
Wise men, 28, 29, 32, 33, 34, 35, 36, 37, 38, 39, 48, 49, 55, 56, 59, 61, 74, 75, 76, 77, 80, 81, 98, 100, 101, 103, 104, 105

www.ingramcontent.com/pod-product-compliance
Lightning Source LLC
Chambersburg PA
CBHW081407080526
44589CB00016B/2487